ENEMY IN THE SKY

Also by Sandy Johnstone:
  ONE MAN'S WAR (TV Series), 1963
  WHERE NO ANGELS DWELL (with Roderick Grant), 1969

ENEMY IN THE SKY

My 1940 Diary

Air Vice-Marshal
SANDY JOHNSTONE,
CB, DFC

PRESIDIO PRESS
San Rafael, California & London, England

Published by Presidio Press of San Rafael, California,
and London, England, with editorial offices at
1114 Irwin Street, San Rafael, California 94901

First American edition 1979

First published in Great Britain in 1976
by William Kimber & Co. Limited
ISBN: 0-7183-0474-8

Library of Congress Cataloging in Publication Data

Johnstone, Sandy.
   Enemy in the sky.

   Includes index.
   1. World War, 1939—1934—Personal narratives, English.
2. Johnstone, Sandy.   3. Great Britain. Royal Air
Force. 602 Squadron—Biography.   4. Fighter pilots—
Great Britain—Biography.   I. Title.
D811.J587 1979   940.54'49'410924 [B]   78-31793
ISBN 0-89141-086-4

Jacket design by Lee Romero

Printed in the United States of America

Contents

List of Illustrations

Foreword

The practice of keeping a diary was severely frowned upon in Official circles at the outset of hostilities, but I reckoned so much was happening after being called up in the third week of August 1939, that it would be a pity if it was not recorded there and then. Besides, I knew how easy it was for memories to dim or become greatly distorted with the passage of time. Not only that, but 602 Squadron had already made its mark in the annals of aviation history, and who could not tell whether it was going to add to its lustre as the years unfolded.

No 602 Squadron was the first Auxiliary Air Force squadron to get into the air in the summer of 1925 and it continued to lead its field for a further two decades before its ultimate disbandment in 1957. For instance, two of its early members, the Marquis of Douglas and Clydesdale (later to become the Duke of Hamilton) and David MacIntyre, succeeded for the first time in conquering Mount Everest in 1932 when they flew converted Wapiti aircraft, renamed Wallaces, on the epic flight sponsored by the late Lady Houston. Neither, alas, is alive today. 602 was the first squadron in the Auxiliary Air Force to be equipped with modern fighter aircraft (Spitfires) and, when hostilities broke out in September 1939, was able immediately to take its place in the front line of the air defences of the country. Indeed, it shared with its Edinburgh colleagues the distinction of bringing down the first enemy aircraft over British soil, when the Germans carried out their first raid over the Firth of Forth on 16th October of that year. It is also for the record, although an occasion better forgotten, that the author has the dubious distinction of having flown the first ever operational sortie done in a Spitfire at night, when it ended on the top of a hill in Renfrewshire. It was a very foggy night!

I am glad now that I preserved a record of the happenings during that fateful year of 1940, for I am still able to describe events exactly as they occurred, without frills and without having to tax a memory fast dimming with the passage of time. The diary shows what we did in the air and on the ground; how we felt; our hopes and our fears; our innermost thoughts. Looking back on the events of that eventful summer as I have recorded them, it is strange how oblivious we were of the significance of the battle which was raging around us and of how ignorant we had been that defeat had not been all that far away. Yet, somehow, we sensed when the tide began to turn in our favour.

There were times of intense action and there were periods of sheer boredom and frustration. But there was plenty of fun, too, and it is all recorded – just as it happened.

Some of the terminology must seem strange nowadays. For instance RDF (Radio Direction Finding) is now better known as Radar. 'The Wireless' is better known as 'The Radio'. And the jargon associated with Fighter Command operations, words which were a daily feature of our lives in those days, need a word of explanation. To name but a few:–

Scramble – take off.

Vector – Steer a course of x degrees.

Angels – height in thousands of feet.

Buster – go as quickly as possible.

Saunter – fly at best cruising speed.

Bandit – aircraft identified as hostile.

Bogey, or X-raid – unidentified aircraft.

Tally Ho – target sighted.

Pancake – return to base and land.

Also, a word of explanation about the various 'States of Readiness' might not go amiss:–

Stand-by – sitting in cockpits ready to start up and go.

Readiness – being able to get airborne within three minutes.

Available – fifteen minutes to get airborne.

Released – released from operations for a specified period.

In a chronicle of this nature, it is inevitable that personalities tend to come and go, when the reader may wonder what has become of them. I have therefore added a short epilogue in an endeavour to complete the picture. However the diary itself is a true record of what it was like to be a fighter pilot during a very important period in our nation's history, when so much depended upon the outcome of the battle in which we had become involved. As such it is definitive, but it is in no way intended as a treatise on the Battle of Britain. In any case, it would not be possible, for none of us realised at the time that a corner of a page of history was being unfolded before our very eyes!

LONDON, December 1975.   A.V.R.J.

The First Four Months

September – December 1939

My job in civilian life in 1939 was as a Navigation Instructor at No 1 Air Navigation School at Prestwick and, as I had been put in charge of training the Volunteers, my duties required me to work most Saturdays and Sundays and I had to take my 'week ends off' on Tuesdays and Wednesdays. Thus it was I found my 'Notice of Calling Out' waiting for me when I returned from a pleasant day's sailing on the Clyde that Wednesday evening, 26th August 1939. The official-looking blue envelope, with 'URGENT' – 'EMBODIMENT' printed on its top left hand corner, contained instructions for me to report IMMEDIATELY to No 602 City of Glasgow Squadron AAF.

I had become a member of the squadron shortly after leaving school in 1934 and was therefore already trained to operational standard, even on the Spitfires, with which the unit had been equipped the previous March, and it was therefore with a certain amount of excitement that I clocked in, as it were, at Abbotsinch that same evening. I was then a Flight Lieutenant in the AAF and had become betrothed to Margaret Croll a few months previously. We were all aware, of course, that a state of tension existed between the British and German nations and had redoubled our efforts to prepare ourselves for the conflict which would surely come.

The squadron spent the month of September under canvas at

Abbotsinch, (now Glasgow Airport) with little else to do but train a batch of new pilots who had been posted to us from the local RAFVR unit. Among those who joined us at this time were Glyn Ritchie, Roddy McDowall and John McAdam. From time to time a Section of three aircraft would be sent off by the Sector Controller at Turnhouse to investigate a plot he was unable to identify, but it was not until the unit had moved to the East coast on 13th October that we saw our first action three days later. The Germans had sent over a force of twelve Ju 88's to attack RN ships anchored off Rosyth and, in company with our Edinburgh colleagues in 603 Squadron (still equipped with Gloster Gladiator bi-planes) managed to account for the first enemy aircraft to be shot down over Britain in the Second World War.

RAF Drem is situated on the East coast of Scotland, about a mile inland from the village of Gullane and not far from the town of North Berwick. Until our arrival there, it had housed a unit from Flying Training Command and most of its permanent staff came from that Command. It must have been something of a shock therefore for these worthy gentlemen to be invaded by a bunch of unruly Auxiliaries who, being Fighter trained, had little time for the spit and polish so necessary in the *ab initio* stages of a cadet's training. Besides, Auxiliaries had a reputation for interpreting King's Regulations in their own way, much to the exasperation of senior officers of the Old School! Then, first blood having fallen to the AAF squadrons in the Firth of Forth raid, two more Regular fighter squadrons were posted in – 111 Squadron under Harry Broadhurst and 72 Squadron, with Ronnie Lees at the helm – so it is hardly surprising that the Station tended to run the permanent staff, instead of the other way round!

The boys soon settled down to their new life style and Christmas passed and was celebrated in conventional ways. The weather turned cold – bitterly cold – and thus it was that, by the time the Old Year was due to be rung out, I found myself the bearer of an aching groin and an inmate of the Station Hospital at RAF Drem. What follows throughout 1940 is recorded in diary form.

January

1st January One expects it to be cold in Scotland during winter, but this is ridiculous! There are real brass monkey conditions both outside and inside the building and even my toothbrush and sponge have frozen solid! Believe it or not, I am in hospital where I think I may have broken some sort of record, for I went to the loo in 1939 and did not emerge from it until 1940! And I have mumps.

It is the second time I have had this disease too, but this time it is not the childish variety I suffered in my adolescence – it is the real thing, and infinitely more painful. Furthermore, my depression was in no way lifted when Archie McKellar reminded me this morning that I am due to be married on the 27th! What a way to start the New Year!

At least the ward was quiet earlier on, for I was the only patient in the Station Hospital at RAF Drem and the staff had pushed off to celebrate Hogmanay, all except McWhirter that is. He, of course, is the junior orderly. So it was disquieting to be rudely awakened from a fitful slumber about two a.m. when the swing doors burst open with a fearful clatter and Cairns Smith was brought in by the medical orderly and unceremoniously dumped on the bed next to mine. My immediate reaction was to regard him as the first of the expected victims of the Hogmanay celebrations, but I was wrong. Cairns had fallen into an empty swimming pool in the blackout and was disclaiming loudly that he must have broken his leg at least.

To add to the misery of the moment, I have had news that Harry Moody's undercarriage folded up on landing this morning and that his aircraft is badly bent, making our sixteenth breakage since war began. However, Harry himself is all right, which is a relief.

Cairns is also relieved, for he has just returned from Edinburgh where he has had an X-ray taken of his leg, with the news that he has only bruised a knee cap. He is to lie up here for a day or two, so at least I will have someone to talk to.

4th January The Station Hospital is not exactly the place in which to lie up for a rest for, what with Cairns's snoring and the bitterly cold conditions, sleep is hard to come by. I am now wearing two pullovers and a pair of woollen mittens and have my heavy service greatcoat spread over the top of the bed and a couple of hot water bottles inside it. Even so, I am still shivering. Furthermore, the food is hardly appetising, as it has to be carried over from the Officers' Mess and is generally congealed on the plates by the time it reaches us.

In spite of this, Cairns seems to be enjoying his enforced lie-up and is reluctant to be discharged. Up till now he has avoided expulsion on the pretext that his trousers were torn when he fell into the pool and they had not yet been returned from the menders, but the nether garments turned up this afternoon and I was very sorry to see him finally limping away. However, I must be on the mend myself as I am now allowed to sit up in a chair, which is at least a change of attitude, if not one of scenery.

I had several visitors this afternoon. Firstly, Fumff Strong looked in to borrow my greatcoat to wear at a service funeral for one of the newly arrived NCO pilots of 72 Squadron who had spun in off a loop and crashed near Haddington, being killed instantly. As our Met man is forecasting warmer weather ahead, I allowed him to take it – reluctantly. Then Harry Broadhurst came by to say he has been promoted to Wing Commander and has been awarded a DFC and he was followed by Nick Nicholson to tell me that 72 Squadron

is moving soon to Church Fenton. I should have asked him whence
he got the news, for the barmaid in The Royal is usually first out
with intelligence of this sort, and she is generally right too!

10th January Managed yesterday to persuade Doc to let me out of
the igloo for a couple of days to allow me time to nip through to
Glasgow to visit the folks. However I stopped off at the Flight office
beforehand to have a session with Findlay Boyd, who has been running B Flight in my absence. Am glad to say there was not much
left for me in the 'Pending' tray; a few flying log books to sign and
the training schedules to check, that was all. Findlay says he likes
our modified filing system, which now consists of two files only, one
headed 'Miscellaneous' and the other 'Mysterious'. Anything
which does not fit easily into either category goes straight into the
wastepaper basket!

It seems our boys are doing more than their fair share of the
readiness states and I found that some of them have been standing
by their Spitfires for days on end, only getting away now and again
to snatch a quick meal in the Mess, and they are having to sleep in
the crew room too. It is the same for the ground crews. Spoke to the
Sector Commander at Turnhouse about it and he assures me 602
will be stood down whenever 609 arrives to take over from the
departing 72 Squadron. I must keep him up to it.

Anxious to reach Glasgow before nightfall as the headlights on
my car were never good at the best of times and now, with blackout
masks fitted, are a positive menace on the open road! So was
pleasantly surprised when the car started up without too much
difficulty, particularly as it has been standing in the cold for so
long. It says much for the old £30 Vauxhall.

Drove first to Margaret's office only to find she was at home, suffering from a severe chill or something, and I found her there,
propped up in bed, wrapped in a cardigan and a woollen shawl and
smelling like a camphorated mothball! Her parents invited me to
stay the night at their flat as my bed at home apparently has been
sent off to have its legs repaired. Had not realised I had been such a
restless sleeper!

Spent this morning making arrangements for the wedding. First called on the Reverend Vernon, minister of Hyndland Parish Church, where the deed is to be done, then drove my prospective mother-in-law to the Central Hotel to order the essentials. Twelve dozen bottles of Veuve Cliquot seems a reasonable supply for our 140 invited guests and it is nice to know that Mr and Mrs Croll intend to despatch their second daughter with such aplomb. My own contribution to this morning's proceedings was to purchase the wedding ring.

Am now back at Drem where I find the boys still maintaining the state and grousing like billyo. 609 Squadron has not turned up yet. The crackling sound when a Spitfire is coming in to land, caused us to look out of the window when we were just in time to watch Alastair Grant tip N on to its nose on the hard ground. I fear some of our lads are still having trouble handling these aircraft, which certainly do call for quick reflexes.

14th January Am pleased to say I passed my medical at the first attempt and went over to the Mess to read the morning newspapers. B Flight was stood down this morning while Marcus Robinson kept the flag flying with A Flight. Had no sooner settled down in a comfortable armchair when we were called to stand-by, as Red Section had been scrambled to intercept a hostile plot. They were already airborne by the time we reached the crew room to don mae wests and climb into our cockpits. However, before we were ordered off, A Flight returned, streaking low across the airfield to show that their gun patches had been blown off. This was to alert the ground crews that they had been in action and that the aircraft would require re-arming. It is important to get this done without delay, for one cannot afford to have aircraft caught unarmed on the ground in case Jerry should attack the airfield as a follow up.

Red Section has had a kill. They intercepted a reconnaissance Heinkel 111 twenty miles off the Fife coast and brought it down in the sea, when Marcus said he saw at least one crew member taking to the rubber lifesaving dinghy. Indeed, Leuchars has just been on the telephone to say they have the pilot of the Heinkel ashore and safely under lock and key. They added that Jerry sent compliments and his congratulations on their good shooting! Cheeky blighter!

Well-off neighbours invited some of us to a party in Edinburgh tonight,which seemed an appropriate way to wind up a successful day. We were dined at the De Guise, and Carl Brisson and Gene Gerrard were in the party. I recognised both from their many film appearances.

15th January Although the temperature has dropped, we have been experiencing a lot of squally snow showers recently, which might, of course, help to keep the Luftwaffe away. However it does not stop convoys from sailing and I began the day leading the dawn patrol over a large assemblage of ships on the point of leaving Methil Bay. Paul Webb, Glyn Ritchie and I took off in darkness and reached them as dawn was breaking. It is one of our jobs to protect the convoys as they pass between the Firth of Forth and the Borders, when our colleagues operating from further south take over, and vice versa.

The tedium of this particular patrol was relieved when the section was ordered to investigate an X-raid approaching from the east at 25,000 feet. Windscreens and canopies became completely frozen up as we climbed through snow filled clouds, and I soon lost visual contact with the other two, when I hoped they had remembered the drill to turn away left and right before resuming their original course two minutes later. We broke clear at 23,000 feet and I called in Glyn, who was some way off to port. However, there was no sign of Paul and I tried unsuccessfully to call him for some time while we continued to search for the bogey. It appeared the plot disappeared from the table soon afterwards and we were ordered to return to base and land.

Glyn was able to keep station during the descent by using the back of a penknife to scrape the frost from his canopy and we broke cloud directly over Leuchars at 2000 feet. There was a Coastal Command Lockheed Hudson aircraft on the runway about to start its take-off run and we watched it gathering speed as it approached the eastern end of the airfield. However, something obviously went wrong for instead of climbing away, the aircraft disappeared into the pine forest in a cloud of dust. Thick black smoke and flames followed, then suddenly everything shot skywards as the depth charges, bombs, ammunition and Very-light cartridges all blew up together. It was like a Brock's Benefit, and yet seemed totally unreal, because we could hear nothing of the drama above the noise of our own engines. It was just like watching a silent film.

Was much relieved to find Paul already on the ground when we landed at Drem. He had had R/T failure and a faulty oxygen supply and had wisely decided to abandon the sortie. We were also glad to learn that the crew of the Hudson had got away with only minor injuries. Such is the luck of the game, I suppose.

18th January The elements have taken over again, as the airfield is now completely snowbound and flying is out of the question. Decided therefore to snatch the opportunity for a quick visit to Glasgow. Archie was sceptical about my chances of getting through in my own car and offered to drive me over in his. I was glad to accept and was duly deposited at my parents' flat in Atholl Gardens where a barrage balloon operates from just outside the front door. Even it was grounded by the weather and was covered with a thick blanket of snow, and I was fascinated to watch its crew throwing ropes over the top of the balloon to clear some of the snow from its envelope. Doubtless it also helped to keep them warm in the very cold conditions.

Took Margaret to see *The Lion has Wings* in the Grosvenor Picture House this evening.

23rd January Charles Keary, our Station Commander, is one of the old school and loves his bit of spit and polish. However, it is not always easy to keep up to his standards, operating, as we do, off a grass airfield which is either a sea of mud or frozen solid, as it now is. Besides, many of our chaps have to live for days on end without any chance of getting out of their clothes and spend more time in the crew room than anywhere else. So, having recently had to endure the rigours of a church parade held in a draughty hangar, no one was very enthusiastic about having to turn out again a few days later for a Station Commander's Parade and Inspection. Efforts had been made to clear just enough snow from the tarmac to accommodate the personnel of three squadrons plus the Headquarters Staff, but a recent fall of rain had turned the surrounding areas into a veritable ice rink.

The highly polished staff car swept round the corner and skidded to a stop opposite the saluting dais where the Group Captain stepped out, immaculately dressed as always. Alas, all we saw of him this time were his legs high in the air as he fell flat on his back at the foot of the dais. The parade was cancelled!

One of the pilots has had a spell of bad luck lately when he started off by putting a Spitfire on its back at Acklington two days ago and tipping another on its nose at Drem yesterday. As if that was not enough, he jolly nearly landed a third aircraft at Drem with its wheels up today, and was only saved from doing so by the quick-wittedness of Bill Scarnell who saw what was happening and managed to fire a warning red Very light across his bows at the last minute, thereby preventing the pilot's third accident within a week. Full marks to Bill, and it provided a classic example of how his alertness won him a VC and an MM during the last war!

Our MT Section was also in the toils this week when one of our drivers skidded a 30 cwt lorry into 'Hannibal', pride of Imperial Airways, which had just landed to deliver the ground crews and equipment for 609 Squadron. However, Captain Peacock was remarkably philosophical about the damage to the leading edge of his machine and was courteous enough to show me over this large aeroplane. It was impressive, too, and can carry forty two passengers in luxury unheard of until recent years. It even boasts a loo! But it was the size of the control column which most impressed me, for it reminded me of a grossly enlarged version of the steering wheel of my father's old Bianchi.

26th January George Reid, who was one of my colleagues at Prestwick before the war, has undertaken to be Best Man at our wedding and I visited Edinburgh yesterday to buy him a small memento of the occasion. I also called on my bank manager at the same time, for I thought it wiser to get such tasks done before the Burns Night celebrations on the 25th, as the boys had arranged to combine them with my traditional pre-marital stag party.

They tell me it was an uproarious dinner although, to be

truthful, I cannot remember much about it. All I know is that I have a mouth like the bottom of a parrot's cage today and feel as if I have been run over by a tramcar. So I was right! I could never have faced my bank manager in this state! Furthermore, I see Donald Jack is sporting a black eye which, they also tell me, I dished out while he and Dunlop Urie were trying to throw me into a cold bath.

31st January Well, the knot is now tied. Naturally, Margaret was disappointed that war time convention deprived her of a white wedding but, nevertheless, she looked absolutely smashing in a bluey-green costume with furry bits round it. I wore uniform of course. Padre Sutherland assisted the Reverend Vernon at the marriage service and nearly deafened us with the lustiness of his singing, for I fear neither Margaret nor I are used to standing face to face with a burly Highland parson at full throttle. Furthermore, George's ministrations with the champagne bottle beforehand had been somewhat liberal, and I found myself bursting to spend a penny in the middle of the proceedings! However, by dint of concentrating hard on the ceremony itself, I was just able to hold out until we reached the vestry to sign on.

Like so many other people of my generation, I seem to have an untold number of family relations, most of whom I only meet at funerals and weddings. Today was no exception. They turned up in droves. I am glad to report that Donald also managed to make it and evoked considerable sympathy from many of my female relatives who immediately assumed his discoloured eye to be part of a legitimate war wound. However, many of the other invited guests were unable to reach Glasgow because of heavy snow falling throughout the night. Thus the ratio of champagne per guest improved considerably and, as the afternoon wore on, I was not surprised to see uncles, aunts and cousins, normally most well behaved and demure, showing considerable lack of restraint when I was carried shoulder high and deposited on the roof of the taxi, whilst Margaret and a number of uninvited inebriates bundled higgledy-piggledy inside it. I was only allowed inside myself when I almost fell off the roof of the car as it swung into Bothwell Street!

Having picked up the Vauxhall from a nearby garage and

deposited confetti from our clothes all over my parents' flat, we set off for Troon on the first stage of the honeymoon. The snow was still falling thickly and it was difficult to see the road ahead, in spite of using an unmasked spotlight. However, by the time we had reached Kilmarnock, I woke up to the fact that I had forgotten to switch on the windscreen wiper and it was an altogether easier journey from there on!

Things became slightly chaotic when we fetched up at the Marine Hotel, for Margaret began by signing the register with her maiden name, thus causing a few eyebrows to be raised nearby. Then suspicions were hardly allayed when I insisted on having the twin-bedded room changed for one with a double bed, although as it turned out, I needn't have bothered! However, we had a more sympathetic reception next morning when our photograph appeared in the local papers.

By now the snow was lying outside to a depth of nine feet and all thoughts of proceeding towards the South had to be abandoned. In fact, we read in the Press that several cars and buses were still missing on the Fenwick Moor road, the same road we had blindly driven over ourselves, and that the Royal Scot was stranded with a trainload of passengers in a snowdrift somewhere on Beattock Summit. It is apparently the worst snowstorm for umpteen years. So we had to resign ourselves to imprisonment at Troon for the next couple of days.

We eventually reached the Prestwick road after digging a passage across a field and made for our old stomping ground, The Orangefield Hotel, where a number of our friends reside, including George. However, we found that George was still marooned in Glasgow. And now, to cap it all, I have gone down with a bout of influenza and Margaret is also sickening for something else, as yet undiagnosed. I am sure there must be more orthodox ways of starting one's married life!

February

6th February The flu bug turned out to be fairly mild but it nevertheless kept me in bed for four days. I sincerely hope I am not going to start off every month in the hands of the medicos this year. Fortunately Margaret recovered quickly and whatever had been threatening her never came to fruition; I expect it was just an attack of excitement, or something. Also George finally got back and took care of the bride whilst less reputable friends took it in turns to visit my sickroom and ply me with a lot of unwanted drinks. David and Prunella Douglas-Hamilton also looked in with news that one of the Navigation School Ansons was missing on a training flight. Prunella (née Stack) is still going great guns with her League of Health and Beauty and is off to do a show with them in London, so I offered to let her have my unused leave warrant, hoping the railway people would not check to see how many Mrs Johnstones there really are!

My temperature returned to normal a couple of days ago, leaving me with nothing worse than a hacking cough, so decided thenceforth to take the cure into my own hands, and went for a stroll on the airfield. I bumped into the Chief Flying Instructor on the tarmac who told me that the Anson had been discovered in Northern Ireland where it had crashed, killing all four occupants. It seems 602 Squadron is not the only outfit involved in the demolition business!

Cranked up the car again on Monday as my leave is due to finish on Wednesday and I considered it prudent to get under way in case we had more snow. As it was, we had to drive to Glasgow via the coastal road as that over Fenwick Moor is still impassable. Indeed there have been drifts of more than twenty feet on Fenwick Moor and the body of a stranded motorist was recovered from it only yesterday while, in another spot, a double decker bus is apparently just beginning to reappear through the top of a snow drift. The coast road was bad enough, and in some parts where the snow had piled up, single lane channels had been cut in it, when one had to drive along a sort of levelled out Cresta Run. Progress was therefore slow and very bumpy. However we eventually fetched up at my parents' place, where we stopped for the night.

Presumably in deference to our newly acquired marital status, Mother and Dad have lashed out on a double divan bed which I found to be decidedly uncomfortable until finding that my side of it had been erected upside down!

10th February Returned to Drem yesterday to find Findlay had taken B Flight to Acklington to carry out firing practice and that he had also been promoted to Flight Lieutenant. I hope that will not mean him being posted from 602, as he is a real stalwart in the flight. However, apart from finding a number of the lads laid low with flu, nothing much else of importance seems to have been happening while I was away. The fierce weather has apparently been affecting all of us.

I took over as soon as the flight returned from Acklington and led Yellow Section this morning when it was sent to investigate a plot approaching from the east. The Squadron Commander, Douglas Farquhar, was already airborne with Red Section and I heard him give the tallyho on his R/T soon after we took off but, by the time we caught up with him, Douglas had scored hits on a Heinkel 111 which by then was making towards North Berwick with thick smoke belching from one of its engines. Circling overhead, we watched it landing, wheels up, on the hill behind the town and three crew members clambering out. These were soon rounded up by the police and handed over to the military, whilst the wounded rear gunner was brought into the Station Hospital at Drem where he died soon after.

When I visited the scene in the afternoon, scores of curious spectators were milling round the crashed Heinkel, but the police were firmly in charge and had managed to prevent would-be souvenir hunters from getting too close, and all its equipment appears to be intact. A number of press reporters were among the crowd and one of them asked me if I realised this was the first enemy aircraft to be brought down on British soil. I had not thought about it until then, although it is certainly the first I have seen at close quarters. Indeed there was something odd about seeing a Heinkel sitting on the ground so near home and I thought at the time that the machine looked strangely fragile and vulnerable, and not half so menacing as it had looked in the air. I made a mental note then to remember this whan I met any more of the blighters upstairs! However, there was a touch of the incongruous about it too, for its tyres had 'Made in Germany' printed on them in English!

14th February Margaret is taking a few days off from work and has come through to spend them at the Farquhars and, as enemy traffic was light, I was able to run over to Edinburgh and meet her off the train at Waverley Station. Having first seen her safely installed with our hosts I then returned to Drem to give McAdam an hour's practice on the Link Trainer but, judging by the unusual number of jerks, squawks and puffing coming from the machine's bellows, I fear he made very heavy weather of it.

Whilst patrolling over Convoy 'Argent' yesterday afternoon we were ordered to go after a Dornier which was reported to be stalking the ships from high above. However it was a fruitless effort which ended up with us chasing our own plots. This sometimes happens when there is a time lag between the plots being co-ordinated in the Ops Room and then being passed to the fighters by R/T, as they have by then become confused with the plots of the fighters themselves. We call this 'ogo-pogoing', which is reputed to have derived its name from the mythical bird, the Greater Ogo

Pogo, because it is such a crafty bird that it is able to fly around in ever decreasing circles until it eventually performs the amazing evolution of flying up its own fundamental orifice, from which advantageous position it continues to throw abuse in the faces of its pursuers!

Another fruitless sortie this morning when we spent an hour and a half combing the skies over Lanarkshire, chasing plots emanating from the Observer Corps. We were disappointed at not coming up with the goods, as information from Observer Corps sources is generally most reliable.

Cairns Smith and Bill Scarnell are both being posted to the Operations Staff at Turnhouse. We will miss them.

18th February It is always pleasant to have a break from the continual routine of convoy patrols and we varied the diet this morning by acting as targets for the Ack-ack boys in the district. The Gunners are always grateful to have live targets on which to operate their new camera gun attachments which provide them with a permanent record of their efforts that can be analysed at leisure. Sometimes we tell them, rather rudely, that we would feel just as safe if they let fly with the real thing, instead of merely taking our pictures! However the Royal Navy is an entirely different kettle of fish, as they tend to operate on the maxim of 'shoot first and interrogate afterwards' and we always insist on having one of our fellows on board when our friends in dark blue choose to practice their shooting against us! Sector Operations sometimes sets up its own form of training too, by using a single Spitfire as a target, whilst the controllers practise vectoring one or two sections of fighters on to it. As a matter of fact, we were involved in such a game last Saturday with Sergeant Babbage acting as target and Paul and I as the interceptors, when the weather suddenly turned sour and we had to beat a hasty retreat for Drem before it clamped down completely. As it was, Paul and I only got down by the skin of our teeth but Babbage, who had only been assessed operational the day before, wrote off his undercarriage on the third attempt at a landing.

Birdie and Claire Saul have taken a cottage at Gullane, which is just down the road from the airfield. While it is nice to have the AOC visiting us now and again, we hope this won't mean he henceforth will be breathing down our necks. However, on reflection, he could hardly be doing that as his Headquarters is at Newcastle, so I expect we will be more likely to have him around at the week ends. We will just have to wait and see! At all events, the Sauls came to supper with the Farquhars this evening, after which we all went to a picture house at Haddington and saw Fred Astaire in *The Story of Vernon and Irene Castle*. Unfortunately Margaret has to get back to her job and returns to Glasgow tomorrow. However Findlay is going on leave in the West and has offered to drive her through.

21st February Douglas Farquhar and I were sent off this morning to take part in a search for a Hurricane reported down in the sea off May Island. A Hudson from Leuchars was already in the area when we got there but neither it nor we found any trace of the missing aircraft or its pilot. Control was unable to give us much information about the mysterious affair and told us they were only acting on a message passed from a ship via the coastguards but, as far as we can ascertain, no one is reported missing from any of the Hurricane squadrons hereabouts. However we had a troublesome return to Drem after the sortie, as a sudden thaw had set in and both Douglas and I nearly tipped our aircraft on their noses in the soft ground. The field is particularly soft at the foot of the slope and this, of course, is where I would have to choose to run into! I just managed to pull the nose up in time before the prop touched the ground.

The AOC rang Douglas, while I was in his house collecting my gear, to tell him he had just been awarded the DFC so, instead of returning to the expected mediocre dinner in the Mess, I was treated to a jolly good celebration meal at the Marine Hotel! Margaret will be furious when she finds out what she has just missed!

22nd February Suffering from a thick head from last night's celebrations, and was therefore none too pleased to be called to

readiness this morning before six o'clock. Ops were reporting
enemy activity in our Sector, but were unable to say exactly
whereabouts. I was on the rota to lead Green Section with Ian
Ferguson and Sergeant Moody whilst Douglas, also feeling
somewhat brittle, said he would take Red Section which had our
only cannon armed Spitfire in it. In the event, Green Section was
ordered off first and was sent to patrol off the Fife coast. Shortly
after getting into position we heard Red Section being vectored
towards St Abb's Head and Douglas giving the tallyho, so we left
our spot and set off at full throttle to join him, and reached the area
in time to watch a Heinkel 111 making a forced landing in a field
nearby, with three Spitfires circling overhead. We were surprised
then to see one of the Spitfires detach itself from the others, lower
its undercarriage and then proceed to land alongside the Heinkel,
but we were even more surprised when the Spitfire suddenly
cartwheeled and ended up on its back. From chatter going on on
the R/T it transpired it was our Squadron Commander who had
come to grief so ignominiously.

However, Douglas is back at Drem again with a stiff neck, three
Lugers and a fascinating tale. He says he had first managed to
silence the Jerry rear gunner and then called in the cannon Spitfire
to do its stuff, but it had unfortunately encountered a gun stoppage
after firing only a few rounds.

However, the Heinkel was already on its way down and Douglas,
being anxious to assess what damage the cannons had inflicted,
and having been unable to attract anyone's attention to the stricken
aircraft because of the isolated area in which it had come down,
decided to intervene himself to prevent the Germans from destroy-
ing the evidence. Instead he found himself trapped under the inverted Spitfire and was only able to free himself from it with help
from the German crew he had just shot down. He thus found
himself alone with three disgruntled adversaries, all armed, none of
whom was willing to give himself up quite so easily.

However, help eventually turned up in the shape of a detachment
of Local Defence Volunteers led by a worthy from the Great War
who, not unnaturally, assumed Douglas was a member of the
Heinkel's crew and tried to arrest him along with the rest. Indeed,

it was only after he was shown the Spitfire lying at the foot of the hill and Douglas had produced an Income Tax form he had received in this morning's post, that the LDV commander began to believe his story. Even so, he says, he was feeling distinctly uncomfortable about his position, for he had managed to persuade the Germans to part with their arms when they saw the troops approaching, and he reckoned these old war veterans would have viewed him with renewed suspicion if they had come across his sizeable armoury! However, all was well in the end and our CO was returned to us with an augmented headache and furious with himself for breaking his aircraft, his first serious mishap since he started flying thirteen years previously.

25th February Spring has chosen to pay an unseasonal visit, for the weather has suddenly turned mild and clear and it is now such a pleasant change to be able to cruise at leisure round the convoys and to be able to see for miles in all directions. Let us hope we have got rid of the dreadful conditions we have been experiencing for the past seven weeks.

Douglas and I drove to Coldingham this afternoon to visit the scene of yesterday's engagement and found we were unable to get closer than two miles to it in the car. In fact having now trudged the distance over very rough ground, I give full marks to these elderly LDV chaps for having reached the scene as quickly as they did.

The Germans had been able to set their aircraft alight before descending the hill to drag Douglas from his wrecked Spitfire and the forward end of it is completely burnt out. However one can see plenty of bullet holes in the after fuselage, although we could find no traces of any damage from cannon fire. As for the Spitfire, I fear it will become a write-off as it is already half submerged in the swamp and I guess its back is broken as well. All told, Douglas has had a lucky escape.

Was surprised to find Findlay in the crew room when we returned, for he is not due back off leave until tomorrow. After checking dates, he was furious when he discovered his mistake and left again in a high dudgeon to spend another night in Glasgow with his wife!

The clocks changed to Summer Time this morning and the Government says it intends it to remain so for the duration of hostilities. I suppose it is a good thing, although I shouldn't think the farmers will like it. Nevertheless it suits us at the moment for the dawn patrol henceforth will set off an hour later than before!

The Station Commander is on the warpath again and has ordered a big clean up all round. He says we can expect an important visitor tomorrow.

28th February Great excitement today. The King has been at Drem and we have all been presented to him.

The entire Station was paraded in squadrons, everyone wearing their best blues and looking unfamiliarly tidy. Even our gas mask cases had to be buffed up! So, after being given a quick briefing by the Station Adjutant on how to bow from the neck if lucky enough to be presented, we stood in ranks waiting for the big moment.

Stuffy Dowding, our C-in-C, Sir Richard Pierse and Birdie Saul were with the Monarch as he came down the lines and spoke to each of us in turn, but I was too overcome by the occasion to remember what was said as we shook hands, although I do remember thinking that the King must also be visiting units of the Fleet as he was in Naval uniform. After the inspection was over, Douglas was called in front of the whole parade when HM pinned the DFC on his tunic. We all felt enormously proud at that moment to see our Commanding Officer being honoured in this way.

The C-in-C remained on at Drem after our Royal visitor had departed and made his own tour of the station, in the course of which he spent some time in our crew room talking to pilots and ground personnel alike. Then Claire and Birdie pushed out the boat and had a number of us to their cottage for cocktails, when Dowding had some nice things to say about our efforts so far. All in all, it has been a great day for the boys at Drem.

The rest of the news seems humdrum after the main event, but nevertheless is not without incident. Firstly, 111 Squadron has upped sticks and gone off to do a stint at Wick, and we hear that they will be replaced by 264 Squadron which is coming north to take a breather after a tough spell operating in France. Secondly, Green

Section was unexpectedly scrambled over Convoy 'Merit' when 609's standing patrol latched on to a Heinkel which they spotted prowling near their charges. And they got it down in the sea off Dunbar too.

March

2nd March Although we were kept at readiness throughout yester-day, nothing happened and we became thoroughly bored. Even the routine shipping avoided coming into the Sector and we passed the time mooning around the dispersal, waiting for business that never came, and eventually reaching the stage when we were almost will-ing the Germans to send something over to tempt us into the air! Strangely enough, it seems to tire the boys just as much when they are not flying and have to hang about the crew room, kicking their heels, playing interminable games of draughts, reading and re-reading the same old magazines or listening to Paul Webb's latest gramophone record 'In the Mood' so often that they even-tually got to know every cadence of every beat in the number! So we were delighted when a party of OTC boys from a school in Dunbar came to look round the Station when some of us were detailed to show them around. They were a nice bunch of lads, most of whom were eager to join up. I just hope they were suitably impressed with the monumental line I shot them as we went from place to place!

Things began to liven up in the middle of the night however when we were awakened by the strident ringing of the Ops telephone about four o'clock and Archie McKellar, George Proud-man and I were all ordered off, one after the other. George flies the

Graeme

Boyd

Self

Webb

Ferguson

Pinkerton

At dispersal, Drem, November 1939.

His Majesty King George VI visits 602 Squadron, Drem, February 1940.

C
Dowding

Charles
Keary

Douglas
Farquhar

H.M.

Wheeldon

George
Pinkerton

Our wedding, 27th Januar[y]
1940, at Hyndland Paris[h]
Church.

(*Below*): Officers of 60[?]
Squadron, taken at Drem i[n]
April 1940 on the departure [of]
Squadron Leader Farquha[r]
back row, left to right: F/[O]
Coverley, F/O Webb, F/[O]
Jack, W/O McIntosh, F/[O]
Grant, F/O McKellar, F/[O]
Ferguson, F/O Ritchie; *fro[nt]
row, left to right:* F/O Uri[e,]
F/L Robinson, S/L Farquha[r,]
F/L Johnstone, F/L Boy[d]

cannon Spitfire. A convoy had reported it was under attack south of St. Abb's Head and, as we raced towards the area, saw a number of bright flashes lighting up the sky ahead, which we assumed to be ack-ack coming up from one of the escorting destroyers. However the fun was over by the time we got there and the raider had pushed off, having apparently failed to score any hits on the ships, although doubtless claiming that he had sunk at least half the British Merchant Navy! Ops had had no early warning of the enemy's approach so we can only presume it slipped in unobserved beneath the RDF cover.

No sooner returned to base to refuel when we were ordered off again, this time to investigate a plot reported to be over Perth but, as before, we saw nothing of the intruder. However, we were ordered to check up on the latest position of the convoy before returning to Drem and, by the time we had reached the Border area, heavy rain storms made our task difficult and it took some time to locate the ships. By then we had been airborne for an hour and a half and George reported he was short of fuel and would have to go down. Fortunately daylight was breaking and he was able to make a wheels-up landing in a field behind Dunbar, but I fear our cannon Spitfire is now out of the reckoning, at least for the time being. Not that it has done much for us anyway!

Was feeling very tired by the time we were released from ops, so missed breakfast and went straight to bed.

6th March The controllers at Turnhouse must be trigger happy these days for they are constantly sending us off to chase spurious plots. In fact, I myself went on three such sorties yesterday when the only thing I came across was one of our own Ansons which had got lost. But these unnecessary excursions are pushing up flying hours to such an extent that routine servicing inspections are coming round so rapidly that the maintenance organisation is in danger of becoming swamped. Ops has therefore agreed to reduce the strength of Sections from three aircraft to two for the time being.

The Adjutant has gone on leave and I have been talked into doing his job while he is away, and I cannot say I am exactly relishing the task. Besides, the filing system seems unnecessarily complicated after the simplicity of our own Flight arrangement, but I had better not alter it, otherwise Fred would have a fit when he returns! However I had to hold an 'Orderly Room' yesterday to hear a charge against one of our MT drivers who had accidentally set fire to a refuelling bowser. I hope I have done the right thing, for I let him off with a caution to be more careful in future.

Douglas looked in to see how I was getting on and showed me a letter he had just received from our Honorary Air Commodore, Lord Stonehaven. Apparently the noble gentleman had met the King recently who had recounted to him the tale of Douglas's encounter with the Germans. According to Lord Stonehaven, The King thinks it terribly funny although I regret to say those in somewhat less exalted circles apparently think otherwise, for Douglas got a hell of a ticking off from them for jeopardising the safety of his aircraft!

10th March Good old Edinburgh! 603 Squadron, which is operating out of Dyce at present, managed to clobber a Heinkel off Wick on Thursday. However things are less active down here and the Luftwaffe has been giving us a miss lately which is probably just as well, for it is allowing me to concentrate on the Adjutant's job, which seems to comprise largely of pushing round the bumff. Nevertheless I was bidden to attend the Station Commander's weekly conference the other day when I found Charles Keary looking as if he had the cares of the world resting on his shoulders. 'Trouble – nothing but trouble!' was how he greeted me, when I realised he was referring to 602 Squadron in particular.

In fact, I got a fair old roasting about all sorts of misdemeanours supposedly perpetrated by the Squadron, ranging through scruffy turnout, a bath plug missing from the airmen's ablutions and even about a dented dustbin which, he inferred, must have been run into by one of our drivers! I gather he is not over-fond of Auxiliaries but I nevertheless thought it strange that we did not touch on any operational matters during the entire meeting.

George Proudman has been to Catterick to pick up another cannon Spitfire, but does not think much of it, as it is apparently throwing quantities of oil all over the place. However, I hope he has more success with this machine than he did with the previous one.

I think the Powers-that-Be must have had a scare the other night, for Group now want us to carry out patrols over the convoys at night as well as by day, although I have not heard reports of any of the ships having been hit in that particular convoy. So I am jolly glad we pressed on with our night training when we did, for we now have a reasonable number of pilots qualified to share the load.

Claire and Birdie have invited Margaret to stay, which is a kind gesture, particularly as it includes me too when I am able to get away. As an appreciative acknowledgement, I undertook to pluck their Selyham terrier, but now wish I hadn't for it will take me weeks of hard brushing to get rid of Sailor's hairs from my tunic!

15th March Fred is back and I was glad to hand over to him and return to more orthodox things. However, as enemy activity was still light, I was able to wheel out the squadron Harvard trainer and take some of the ground crews for a joyride. These fellows have very little opportunity to get into the air nowadays and were much better off in that respect when the squadron was equipped with multi-seater aircraft such as Harts and Hinds. That, of course, was before our role was changed from being a light bomber squadron to that of a single seater air defence unit. At the time of the transition we were all impressed by the manner in which our ground personnel accepted the change, which must have been a disappointment to many of them, and soldiered on in the same old loyal way. They don't complain – much!

In view of the lull I was given three days off, and took Margaret through to Glasgow to see her parents. While there we took in a theatre, The Pavilion, when Margaret's sister Ruth and her husband Jim joined us. Wilson, Kepple and Betty topped the bill, being ably supported by another screamingly funny turn, a gentleman called Noni the Clown. Jim has just acquired a new car, a Silver Eagle Alvis, but its lines have been somewhat marred by a bash in the front collected when he collided with a pedestrian in the blackout. Not quite so funny!

I am afraid Johnny Citizen is still not taking the war very seriously, for we had a practice air raid alert as we were coming out of the theatre and no one took a blind bit of notice! I can't help feeling it is a dangerous attitude, for the real thing could very well happen one of these days.

The *Glasgow Herald* reports this morning that Douglas has been promoted to Wing Commander, so I presume it will mean a change of Commanding Officers. Wonder who he will turn out to be?

20th March Margaret and I returned to Gullane last night to find Douglas still in command but with news that he is soon to go to Martlesham Heath as Station Commander. I wonder how he will like Suffolk. So far there is no news about his successor.

Birdie's week-end was interrupted this morning when Mickey Mount, his ADC came in with news of an air raid on Scapa Flow, so I drove the AOC to the Ops Room to find out the score. Apparently it was not a very heavy raid and damage is confined to a few shore installations and none of the ships has been hit. Mickey later took me for a ride in the AOC's Vega Gull which was more like flying in a saloon car than in an aeroplane. One can even carry on a reasonable conversation while in flight.

We also had a visit by the Press yesterday when Drem was swarming with reporters and cameramen, all vying with one another to get the best stories. I just hope they took some with a pinch of salt for, from what I overheard some of the chaps telling them, their tales of adventure and valour outdid everything that McCudden and Ball had collectively done during the whole of the last war! I was detailed to escort Ted Yoxhall of *Flight* who asked me many searching questions, the answers to which I knew all too few. However, most seemed satisfied with the visit and were particularly impressed by Red Section's mock attack on two visiting Blenheims. So were we for that matter, for it was a ruddy dangerous performance! Things returned to normal after they had gone.

I fear our accident-prone pilot has been up to his old tricks again for, as the aircraft were being dispersed for the night, he managed to taxi my Spitfire into another parked nearby, fortunately without doing a great deal of damage to either. However, I have had a word with the CO about having him transferred elsewhere, for he has obviously got a jinx on him here.

A Hampden bomber landed at Drem last night, having lost his way and run low on fuel, when returning from a raid on the German naval base at Kiel. As this is just the sort of thing to prod Jerry into making a follow-up raid, we deemed it advisable to spread our off-state aircraft further afield and I took B Flight to Turnhouse for the night, whilst 609 Squadron bedded down at Grangemouth. A Flight remained at Drem to keep the overnight state.

25th March As Marcus and his lads had been on duty throughout the night, B Flight undertook the dawn patrol on its way back from Turnhouse on Thursday morning. 609 were weather bound at Grangemouth. There was an Intelligence report waiting for us when we got down at Drem to say that, as a number of German beacons were active in our area, we could expect the tempo of operations to build up within the next few days. Consequently we have been kept at a high state of readiness although the promised onslaught has not yet materialised. Indeed, I calculate that we have now been kept at readiness for seventy three out of the last one hundred and thirteen hours and some of us are beginning to feel the strain. In fact, Paul was looking so completely whacked yesterday I sent him to see the MO who has put him off flying for the next three days and told him to take a complete rest.

In view of the threat of increased enemy attention, Douglas suggested we set about finding better ways of dispersing our surplus aircraft. This led us to take a look at Macmerry, the one time headquarters of The Edinburgh Flying Club, as it lies not far from Drem and would be comparatively easy to service from there. Besides we had been told that it was no longer in use as a flying field. However, when Douglas and I drove over to have a look at it, we found the field was being extended and that it was swarming with workmen of one sort or another. Nevertheless we agreed to bear it in mind for the future, particularly as the clubhouse itself would make an admirable dispersal.

Archie was scrambled in the middle of the night to go to aid of a convoy being threatened off Montrose, and stayed with his charges to the limit of the Spitfire's endurance. He had no longer returned to refuel when word came through that the convoy had been attacked and one of the ships was on the point of sinking. It really was infuriating for him and Archie's reactions were predictable, but alas hardly printable!

The big news is that George Pinkerton is coming back to the squadron to take over from Douglas. In fact, he only left us last November to become CO of another fighter squadron, and up till then had been my Flight Commander. He has a reputation for being somewhat taciturn and, in fact, had become known as 'Grumpy', as it had been the obvious choice for him when we chose to have the names of the seven dwarfs painted on the sides of our aircraft at the beginning of the war. I wonder whether the same held good for me however, for mine had 'Bashful' painted on it!

27th March We have had a lot of early morning frost lately and Harry Moody has broken a collar bone by slipping while climbing into a Spitfire. However I am glad he has been able to get away with Pat Lyall for his Commissioning interview with the AOC and I hope they pass the test, as they are both excellent fellows. At the other end of the scale, as it were, the pilot has been adjudged responsible for the recent taxying accident by the Court of Inquiry, and is to be posted soon from the unit.

Flew on the dawn and dusk patrols today, both over convoys entering and leaving the Firth of Forth. Encountered some naval units off May Island on the latter sortie which were carrying out firing practice against a drogue target. They apparently got their sights a bit mixed up, for they took a few pot shots at me as well. However they sent their apologies later!

31st March The problem of how to disperse off-state aircraft is still exercising us for, we argue, it is beyond our resources of ground equipment to move portions of the squadron into strange airfields which have no Spitfire services to offer. So we are looking again at better ways of spreading the aeroplanes around Drem itself and, after hoofing it around the field all morning, have finally decided to scatter them along the eastern boundary of the airfield from the petrol farm southwards, realising of course that it will entail a long walk for some. However, exercising my privilege as a Flight Commander, Q will occupy the site nearest to the crew room!

I flew Donald Jack to Turnhouse this morning in the Magister to collect one of our Spits which was having a new prop fitted. As the North Berwick Heinkel is still lying in one of the hangars there, I took the opportunity to have a closer look at the machine. I understand the Air Ministry is allowing us to keep one of the panels off it as a souvenir, which will make a worthy addition to the Squadron's trophies.

George Proudman flew his replacement cannon job into a windsock today while doing a formation take-off with Alastair Grant. Fortunately the aircraft is not badly damaged but he was nevertheless lucky to get away with it. I later air tested another replacement Spitfire which I found to be servicable except for the undercarriage handle, which almost came away in my hands! As a matter of fact these pump handles are a constant source of worry, especially for new pilots, for the sequence after take-off is strange, to say the least. One has to move the left hand from the throttle lever to the control column to leave the right one free to waggle the lever. However, this is an unfamiliar manoeuvre for the new boys, who invariably start both hands waggling together with the result that they climb away with a violent see-saw motion. In fact, it is easy to spot someone doing his first solo on Spitfires from this strange switchback take-off which looks more like something out of a fun fair!

B Flight has flown more than 300 hours this month.

April

4th April The boys must have been even more tired than I thought, for the first of the month passed with none perpetrating any Fool's Day tricks. In fact, the only person who seems to be playing tricks these days is The Almighty himself who has varied our weather diet again by producing gales to contend with. It has been blowing very hard these last few days, with gusts up to 50 kts and both Archie and I had to patrol in the dead of night during the worst of it! We managed to cope all right but we both remarked on the effect the strong wind had on the paraffin landing flares, for they looked more like a row of welder's blow lamps than a normal flare path. In fact, it was possible to hear the roar of the flames when one stood close to them.

There was another raid on Scapa Flow a few nights ago when some twenty Do 17's came over, in the course of which the Ack-ack boys got one down and damaged a second. Apparently this lamed duck also had to come down, when the German pilot mistook a Q-site for a flarepath laid out over the sea and crashed on dry land, expecting to ditch in the water. When the soldiers arrived to pick them up, they found the Jerry crew of four sitting in a rubber dinghy beside the remains of the Dornier! Gosh, they must have thought the Scottish water was *very* hard indeed!

29 Squadron is about to join us at Drem and, as they fly Blenheims, should be able to give considerably more bite to the night patrols with their long range twin-engined performance and a crew of two. The arrival of the squadron was preceded by a visit from another Imperial Airways giant, this time 'Scylla', bringing in its ground crews and special equipment. 'Scylla' was to stop at Drem overnight and, having refuelled the thirsty monster, her ground crew was in the course of picketting down the aeroplane when a particularly violent gust of wind caught her broadside on, when 'Scylla' rolled slowly on to her back accompanied by fiendish sounds of tearing metal and snapping flying wires, whilst the two aircrew members still inside scampered up the inner wall and on to the roof as she assumed an inverted position. What happened next was like the Charge of the Light Brigade as everyone nearby grabbed empty tins, bowls, jam jars, teapots – anything which would hold liquid – in which to catch the petrol as it flowed from 'Scylla's' recently fuelled tanks. Everybody was intent on augmenting their meagre petrol ration and I even saw some of maintenance chaps rolling out a fifty gallon oil drum which I thought showed commendable enterprise! Jolly good luck to them! The two occupants trapped inside were eventually released from their lofty prison, but not until the last drop of petrol had stopped flowing!

George Pinkerton arrived today and immediately disappeared into handover consultations with Douglas, who emerged from them in time to come with me on the dusk patrol, his last sortie with the Squadron. I am sorry we could not find anything for him to clobber on this occasion for it would have made a fitting farewell present for him after thirteen years with 602. Douglas joined the unit in 1927.

Ian Ferguson and Paul Webb unfortunately missed the farewell dinner we gave for the Farquhars in The Royal this evening, for they have had to go to Montrose to bolster up the 603 Flight which is temporarily short of aircraft.

9th April I missed Douglas Farquhar's actual departure from Drem as I was airborne chasing a suspect plot at the time. What made it more annoying was that I never caught up with it!

Margaret is back at Gullane again spending a few days with

Claire, so I took both girls to Edinburgh last night for dinner and to
see a picture. It was a film with Arthur Askey and Richard Mur-
doch in it called *Band Waggon,* and we enjoyed it enormously.
Claire slept like a log in the back to the car on the way home which
I took to be a compliment to my driving and not the result of a sur-
feit of our boring company!

Listening to the news bulletin on the wireless at midday today
when it was announced that Germany had just invaded Denmark
and Norway and that Britain had pledged military aid to both
countries. We are naturally wondering if this portends the end of
the 'phoney' war.

As the Squadron is on stand-down this evening Margaret, Claire
and I went for a walk over the golf course. It has been beautifully
clear all day and it was possible to see for miles from the top of the
hill. In fact, we could see as far as Methil where another large convoy is assembling.

Rumour has it that 602 Squadron might become involved in the
fighting in Scandinavia and that we may be moving from Drem
soon.

13th April There are reports of heavy fighting taking place in and
around Norway and that the Allied forces have retaken Bergen and
Trondheim. The Royal Navy is much involved, of course, and must
have been in the thick of things, for we hear HMS *Hunter* has been
sunk in the Skaggerak and that HMS *Hardy* has had to be beached
in Naarvik Fiord. It seems as if the starting pistol has really gone off
this time, and its effect hasn't half woken up the chaps! I have never
seen the Station shooting range so popular, as everyone is trying to
get in some much needed small arms practice, especially on the
revolver range, as a .38 Smith and Wesson is the only weapon we
are given for our personal protection! Those earlier rumours have
been confirmed too, and 602 Squadron is to move tomorrow; one
flight to Dyce, near Aberdeen, the other to Montrose, a little
further south and, for once, this news did not come from behind the
bar in The Royal!

Our new CO has detailed A Flight to go to Montrose and me to
take B Flight to Dyce, where he says he will join us with the Order-

ly Room staff. George Pinkerton and I therefore nabbed the Station Magister and flew to both bases to carry out a recce this afternoon. I can't say I think much of A Flight's new billets, but it looks promising for B Flight, as we will have the use of the clubhouse premises of the Aberdeen Flying Club.

14th April A Flight got away at eight a.m. and we followed three hours later, having had to keep the state going at Drem during the swop-over. For the time being our place at Drem is being taken by 603 Squadron which is apparently coming in to undertake much needed night flying training, which they have been unable to carry out at Dyce and Montrose. But not for us the luxury of an Imperial Airways airliner. No fear. The ground crews had to find their own ways to the new destinations by bus, train, lorry or private car. Nevertheless they all appear to have fetched up at the correct destinations, so maybe this is a good time to take stock of our new base.

Dyce is another grass airfield, very soft and very muddy, and it appears it has had a lot more snow and rain falling on it than on Drem. Indeed, conditions for Spitfires are dreadful and it is only possible to land along the camouflage strips which have been painted across the field in an attempt to fool the enemy into believing they are natural hedges. However the tar based paint binds the loose ground together to a certain extent, which should be a godsend for us. Funnily enough, the muddy conditions don't seem to bother the resident squadron whose Anson aircraft just squelch through the muck.

Things are generally primitive from the point of view of operating a fighter defence system in the area as we are lacking most of the sophistication we enjoyed further south. For instance, the RDF Chain does not extend beyond Dundee and we will have to rely on Coastguards to provide us with information about aircraft movements, and even this will have to be passed over the normal GPO telephones. To make matters worse, the only telephone we have is in the CO's office! However, we are told plans are afoot to build an operations centre of sorts sometime in the future, but nothing appears to have been done about it so far. Gee whizz!

The clubhouse from which we will be operating is situated on the opposite side of the aerodrome from the Messes and maintenance hangars and it would seem we will have to become largely self-supporting for feeding and bedding, at least for the stand-by crews. However, there is a friendly Station Commander in Finlay Crerar who is a past CO of the Aberdeen Auxiliary Air Force squadron and is himself an Auxiliary.

Crerar was not slow to visit us and offered us his full co-operation and promised to see us right. However, he sounded a note of caution about Mr Ghandar Dowar who is retaining an office in the clubhouse buildings. Mr Dowar apparently owns the property and says he intends to go on running a little airline with which he used to maintain a service to Norway before the outbreak of hostilities. However it looks as though that destination will have to be taken off his schedules for the time being and it is a matter of conjecture what destinations he will be able to serve now. At all events, we have been counselled to be diplomatic in our dealings with him and to remember that Mr Dowar is also a Member of Parliament! So Mr Dowar MP will remain with us in the clubhouse building.

Heavy snow is falling as I write this and B Flight has been stood down until tomorrow morning.

18th April The weather has been appalling during the past few days and no flying has been possible, so we spent our time settling in and getting to know the layout of the Station. The frequent heavy snow showers eventually turned to sleet and the airfield has now been reduced to one vast quagmire. Indeed we have been going around with fingers crossed hoping the enemy will not learn of our predicament, for it would not be easy to operate off such conditions if we were called upon. We thought Ops Control was kidding therefore when two aircraft were ordered off this morning to patrol Lossiemouth at Angels 2. Someone had reported seeing a Ju 88.

Findlay Boyd and I took off in a cloud of muddy spray and reached the area in ten minutes but, as we approached Lossiemouth, came to the conclusion that the authorities there must have been holding an aerial carnival or something of that sort, for there were no fewer than three Oxford trainers, two Whitley bombers and two

Anson patrol aircraft all circling round the town together. There was nothing about which resembled a Ju 88.

Being out of range of Turnhouse's R/T we had to use our discretion about the validity of the original sighting and I was about to turn back to Dyce when we spotted an eighth aircraft, which certainly looked like a Ju 88, cavorting at sea level some distance from the coast. I shouted tallyho to Findlay, switched the firing button to the 'on' position and gave chase. As we closed with the target it suddenly swooped up ahead of us, displaying a large pair of RAF roundels as it passed in front. This puzzled us, for it still looked like a Ju 88, and I was relieved to hear Findlay was equally nonplussed. At moments like this, one wished one had spent more time studying aircraft recognition! We continued to circle around for a while, undecided what we should do next, when the target got fed up with our unwelcome attention and turned towards Kinloss where it landed. We returned to Dyce.

When I got through on the phone to the Station Ops officer at Kinloss, he told me he had had two irate pilots standing alongside him who said did we blankety blank not know a long nosed Blenheim when we saw one! I have now suggested to our Intelligence Officer that he arranges a series of lectures on Aircraft Recognition as a matter of urgency! I also arranged for George and me to call on some of the Coastguard Stations this afternoon, for it was high time we tied up aircraft sighting measures with them.

However, before we left the Station, reports began coming in that three fishing trawlers were being attacked off Buchan Ness and Green Section was sent to deal with it. Although they searched the area thoroughly they not only failed to find anything hostile, but failed to find the trawlers in question. Conditions on the ground were bad when they arrived back and both Spitfires skidded off the camouflage strip, ending up travelling sideways and, as one of the Ansons had also got bogged down, we thenceforth put Dyce unserviceable for Spitfires and arranged for the A Flight boys at Montrose to carry the can.

George and I visited a number of Coastguard Stations by road – Kinnaird's Head, Muchalls, Girdle Ness and The Bullers of Buchan – all fine sounding names and manned by great fellows who were as keen as mustard to help. 603 Squadron had already got a system working with them whereby the coastguard chappies put out out a large letter T in front of their station whenever they spotted an enemy aircraft, with the head of the T pointing in the direction in which the aircraft had last been seen travelling. In fact 603 had caught the Heinkel off Wick using this system, so we reckoned that it must be good. Furthermore we learned that the GPO had already promised to give facilities for putting through direct calls from the coastguard stations to our dispersal, when we would fly straight to the station making the call and take up the chase from there. It all sounded simple. So simple that it obviously works. Heath Robinson please note!

25th April Conditions at Dyce have been slow to improve and the only flying activity which has been possible in the past few days was when Harry Moody and I managed to stagger into the air to investigate a report of ships being attacked off Stonehaven. In the event, these turned out to be a few Naval units carrying out gunnery practice, news of which we would probably have learned in advance if we had had the services of a proper Operations Room.

Marcus Robinson turned up on Tuesday evening to tell us he has just been given command of 616 Squadron at Leconfield and he brought with him enough champagne to float a battleship. We were therefore able to congratulate him in an adequate fashion, after which we were just able to send our congratulations to Dunlop Urie on taking over A Flight from Marcus!

There was a whale of a flap this morning when Paul and I were sent off to intercept an unidentified plot approaching from the east. Unfortunately the RDF cover petered out before it came within our range and we were also severely hampered by a thick mist hanging off the coast, so it was not surprising we made no contact with the intruder. But it was just as well, for although the aircraft was German, an Arado seaplane in fact, it had been pinched from under the noses of the Jerries by three adventurous Norwegians who had managed to start it up and fly it to within a few miles from our coast before landing and taxying it into Peterhead harbour with nothing more sophisticated than an old school atlas as a navigation aid!

Ian Ferguson motored to Peterhead to bring back the crew and told us he was surprised the Arado had got as far as it did, for in his opinion it looked a pretty clapped out machine. The captain was a giant of a man dressed in lumberjack's clothes and wearing heavy skiing boots, whilst his two companions were rigged out in old sports jackets and crumpled flannel trousers.

As they came into the clubhouse I was met by a massive hand outstretched in greeting and a booming voice announcing that its owner was Johannsen.

'Johnstone', I replied, whereupon I was nearly felled by a friendly clap on the back as our guest pronounced that 'Ve mosst be brodders den!'

From that moment on I became his mentor – his 'brodder' – and we all took an instant liking to these great fellows. And how they love our whisky! Finlay Crerar is now taking care of them in the Mess while the Intelligence Officer is fluttering around like a demented goose. The poor chap has been trying for hours to get a coherent story out of them, a task which is becoming more difficult as the contents of every tumbler disappear down the grateful gullets!

27th April Things are not going well for us in Norway and Bomber Command aircraft have been very active over there on most nights. Naturally many make for airfields along the Moray Firth rather than having to face the long haul back to their bases in Lincolnshire and further south when they come back from the other side, but the unexpected influx of nightly traffic is causing untold trouble with our Coastguard link-up, as every movement is conscientiously reported by them along the entire line of stations. And these Coastguard chaps are nothing if not thorough! For instance, John MacLean of the Bullers of Buchan insists on spelling out his name every time he calls up and will not get off the line until our fellow spells out his name in return. Of course, by the time these pleasantries have been gone through and we log the message that, 'Ah've got an aeroplane here. Ah canna see it but ah can hear it. It's gaein' buzz buzz. Guid nicht tae ye!' that particular plot is already two stations further along the line and the next one has arrived to take its place! What price Heath Robinson now?

The weather is still against us and our Norwegian friends are weatherbound at Dyce for the time being. Fortunately the stocks of malt are holding out against the onslaught, but I hear the Bar Officer has already paid a visit to the suppliers to plead for an increase in the allocation! When conditions improve they have been cleared to fly the Arado to the flying boat base at Helensburgh and we have been detailed to give them air cover to the West coast. I sincerely hope that everyone en route has been advised about the flight, for the wretched machine still carries its German markings!

In fact the weather is taking its toll all over the district, and we are continually receiving reports of aircraft having forced landed about the place. Only yesterday we picked up Bing Cross from Kintore who had landed there due to bad weather whilst on his way to Norway to recce possibilities for taking 46 Squadron across. We sent a car for him and had him driven to Invergordon where he was able to pick up a Sunderland flying boat, which eventually took him over.

30th April Five workmen and a load of wooden planks arrived this morning which signalled the beginning of an Ops Room. These were followed by a number of GPO engineers who, between them, created such a din with their hammering that I was glad of an excuse to get out of the building for a while to deliver a lecture to the local Ack-ack boys who are billetted in the Beach Pavilion at Aberdeen. I spoke to them about Fighter Operations!

Bing Cross has just returned from Norway and says it will be impossible to take his squadron into Central Norway as he had hoped, as the place is already full of Germans. However, he hopes to join Baldy Donaldson's Gladiators which are now operating off the fiords which are frozen over at this time of the year. He said they had a hairy ride back in the Sunderland which was attacked by a number of Heinkels and a Me 110, but the Sunderland tail gunner had accounted for the latter. It was reported to have gone down in a fiord.

There is no doubt that these fellows have their backs to the wall over there and Baldy apparently lost no less than eighteen

Gladiators when the fiord off which they were flying was bombed by the Germans and many of the parked aircraft fell through the smashed ice. Bing reckons they will welcome his squadron of Hurricanes!

May

2nd May The enemy must be using some of the captured airfields in Norway, for there has been a noticeable increase in the amount of hostile activity against targets in the far north, especially against the Naval installations at Scapa Flow, where many mines have been laid from the air. Naturally we have spent many hours chasing the blighters, but without success because of the lack of plotting information and the continuing spell of bad weather. I myself have done two night sorties recently but am most unhappy about the condition of the airfield and we will have to confine the night patrolling to those we know are capable of coping with it.

The weather is taking its toll elsewhere too and only last night a Whitley bomber flew into a hillside nearby killing five of the eight crew members outright, whilst the other three are very seriously injured in hospital in Aberdeen. The Whitley had been bombed up for a raid and the whole shemozzle went up on impact and it is a miracle any of its crew survived. Also a Henley piled up near Huntly this morning killing both occupants. We felt the full force of this particular tragedy as we actually caught sight of the aircraft momentarily as it turned through the wispy tails of the low cloud, when the pilot obviously failed to spot Dyce almost directly below him. To make matters worse, his wife was standing on the tarmac with us waiting to pick up her husband and saw the whole thing happening. As soon as Finlay Crerar heard about it, of course, he came across and took charge of the poor girl who was completely bowled over by the tragedy.

The news from Norway is grim and our forces are being pulled out from there as quickly as possible and Bomber Command has stepped up its efforts even more. We find it frustrating to be so close and yet not able to lend a more positive hand. We tried marking out a strip on the airfield corresponding with the dimensions of the deck of an aircraft carrier and proved we could operate Spitfires off one at a pinch without the use of arrester gear, but our offer to do so was met with a courteous refusal on the grounds that Dowding says he cannot afford to throw away any more fighters.

We are to have new markings on our aircraft. Yellow rings are to be painted outside the roundels on the fuselage, and vertical red white and blue flashes are to be emblazoned on the tail fins. Also the undersides of the Spitfires will be painted pale blue instead of the present pattern of half black and half white. As Q was already overdue for an inspection, I flew her to Drem this afternoon to have the whole job done at once, and brought back S which has just come from the maintenance hangar.

George and I have invited our wives to join us in Aberdeen for a few days and spent this evening touring the district to find suitable stabling for them. We have settled for Woodside House which is only a seven minute drive from our dispersal.

7th May The girls reacted promptly and turned up on Saturday when we reckoned they must have been keen to come, for they did not even ask us to refund their railway fares! Fortunately there is a lull in the activity at present and we were therefore able to spend some time with them. We started by taking them on a motor tour of the local coastline when we also took the opportunity to pay our respects to the crew of yet another Coastguard Station. This particular look-out post had a beautiful stretch of sands nearby and we spent a happy hour or two on the beach. Alas, we had neither spades nor pails with us and the weather was much too cold for bathing, so we settled for a paddling session before taking them back to dispersal for afternoon tea, where the injection of feminine company was much appreciated. Everything appears so much more normal when girls are around and it is a pity they cannot stay longer with us.

Jackie Hoyle runs the Station Flight, which consists of four Tiger Moths, and he has started to mount his own form of dusk patrols with them. He gets the aircraft to cruise up and down the coast looking for anything suspicious but, as these little training aircraft carry neither wireless nor armaments, I am not very clear what he intends to do if one of his charges comes up against a Heinkel or a U-boat! However it shows the right spirit and I offered to do the odd trip for him when not otherwise engaged, for it was an interesting diversion and gave an opportunity to take more ground crews for a ride. As it turned out, I found it can be mighty cold flying in an open cockpit at 4000 feet!

Our Ops Room is beginning to take shape and we now have a battery of no less than twenty-three telephones laid out in a row. The GPO says it does not have a proper switchboard to give us yet, so we have, instead, a separate telephone to Sector, Group Headquarters, the Coastguard Stations and so on. However, utter chaos occurs when any of them rings for it is difficult to tell which one of the twenty-three it is. One tries to track it down by running up and down the line until the live one is reached but, when more than one instrument goes off at the same time, the system reveals its limitations and often ends up with the wrong handpieces being put down on the wrong instruments. In fact, Archie McKellar was caught out in the fankle last night when this happened for, instead of delivering a ticking off to a NCO in the Sergeants' Mess as he thought, he found himself giving an almighty rocket to the AOC.!

10th May We had a practice air raid alert on the Station yesterday which would have been quite funny if it had not been so darned uncomfortable. The local rules said we had to sit in our aircraft wearing tin hats whilst the ground personnel took shelter in a nearby ditch, but this turned out to be half full of water. Fortunately there was an airmen's dance in the Auxiliaries' Town Headquarters in the evening and the chaps had to change their clothes anyway! As a matter of fact, some of the officers went along as well to give it support and a good evening was had by all. The beer was good and plentiful and so were the girls, but the atmosphere inside the hall could be cut with a knife. Nevertheless we stuck it out to the very end.

Harry Moody and I chased a bogey this morning, but all Ops could tell us about it was that it reported to be flying at 2000 feet somewhere between Bell Rock and Fraserburgh! Because of the height factor we reckoned it was unlikely to be hostile and were therefore not surprised when we intercepted an Oxford Trainer off Stonehaven, whereupon Control ordered us to make it land at Dyce to account for itself. Harry took up station on one side of the trainer whilst I did likewise on its other side and made our intentions pretty clear – or so we thought! However all we got in reply was a cheery wave from the pilot while the Oxford continued on its merry way! However, it seemed to satisfy Control, although our own feelings were decidedly ruffled that our efforts should have been so contemptuously brushed aside!

Wads of signals have been arriving all morning and the telephones have also been red hot. Apparently Germany has now invaded Holland and Belgium and several targets in Northern France have been singled out for heavy air attacks. As a result, all leave has been cancelled forthwith and anyone already away is to be recalled immediately. On top of this we hear the aircraft carrier *Glorious* has been sunk in the North Sea whilst evacuating troops and aircraft from Norway, and that Baldy Donaldson has gone down with it along with most of his squadron. However we also hear that Bing Cross is among the few survivors and that he has been picked up suffering from severe frostbite in his legs and feet. It is now beginning to look as though the war has really hotted up.

14th May The Ops Room is nearly ready and additional personnel to man it have begun to arrive, but goodness knows where they are all going to fit in, for our space is already somewhat cramped. A teleprinting machine turned up yesterday, along with an attractive little WAAF to work it. She seems a rather demure young girl and, I should imagine, has only recently left school. At any rate, she was

frightfully embarrassed when some of the lads who had been sleeping at dispersal wandered in in their pyjamas. However we got a
better reception from her once we shaved and turned up ap-
propriately clad in uniform.

The poor girl sat by her machine throughout the day with absolutely nothing to do, and it was only when a Post Office engineer
turned up this evening and asked why she was sitting there, that it
came to light that the other end of the system was not yet connected
up. However, about an hour after she had left in a dudgeon, with
her pretty little nose high in the air, the wretched instrument
stuttered into life and a higgledy-piggledy jumble of letters and
figures started to appear on the paper scroll. Archie waited until
the machine came to rest then, using his one finger technique,
laboriously enquired whether the operator at the other end was a
blonde or a brunette. The machine spat back the message that it
was an airman!

Twenty Norwegian Air Force officers have now turned up in the
Mess, having got away from their country in one of our destroyers.
They bore tales of fierce fighting and of the stout resistance being
put up by the locals against overwhelming odds and, to a man, are
keen to get back into the fray. These Norwegians are splendid
fellows and we are lucky to have them as allies. While we were talking to them, a panic call came in from a highly strung lady in Aberdeen who was sure she had just seen a party of German
paratroopers landing on the sea front, but even our Norwegian
visitors, who are used to this sort of thing, reckoned such an event
was unlikely to happen in daylight without some sort of warning
beforehand! However, some of our pilots have been reporting odd
things happening to their R/T messages, so I took off in Q to hear
for myself and discovered that some transmissions were indeed being jammed. I was interested that it only appeared to affect
operational messages but all I could do about it was to report the
circumstances to Group and to let them try to sort it out.

It remains operationally quiet at Dyce in spite of all that seems to
be happening elsewhere. Heavy fighting is reported throughout Belgium, Holland and Luxembourg and the Government
has cancelled the Whit holiday in view of the worsening situation.

Ian Ferguson hit a boundary marker whilst coming in to land this evening and has knocked the tail wheel off his Spitfire.

19th May One can hardly believe it! We have been sitting outside the clubhouse, basking in warm sunshine, and someone has come across deck chairs so that we could take full advantage of the improved conditions. In fact, it is difficult to realise there is a war on and that our forces on the Continent are fighting with their backs to the wall. The wireless has been talking of a ding-dong struggle going on around the River Meuse but, wherever it is happening, the conflict seems to be keeping the Luftwaffe fully occupied, for it is certainly leaving us well alone up here. Glyn, Archie and I therefore took ourselves into Aberdeen to see a picture. It was *Destry Rides Again* with James Stewart and Marlene Dietrich in it and we thought how strange it was to watch a German actress performing here at a time like this.

A battalion of Highland soldiers has arrived on the Station to defend the place and, at first, it gave us a sense of pride that the powers-that-be should deem us sufficiently important to care so much for our safety. However we are now not so sure of our status, as the entire ground defence seems to be concentrated on guarding the other side of the airfield!

Dunlop has been on the phone from Montrose to tell us that Hector MacLean was run into by a Master trainer this morning when taxying to the take-off point. Apparently both aircraft have been written off, as the Master was loaded with practice bombs which exploded on impact. It is fortunate the aircraft was not loaded with the real thing, otherwise I fear we would have had a vacancy for another pilot! As it was, both pilots escaped unhurt.

Our Ops Room is almost complete and has a very businesslike air about it. However the GPO has forgotten to install the Ops B line – the most important line of all! No doubt it will be finished one day!

I fear diplomatic relations with Ghandar Dowar were severely strained this morning as a result of a careless mistake by one of our airmen. The guns of a Spitfire were being lined up against sighting markings painted on the door of the hangar when the clot of an armourer accidentally pressed the firing button, causing all eight Brownings to spew lead straight through the building, The fusillade knocked the hat off an airman who was working on a Spitfire inside the hangar and continued through the clubhouse kitchen, then on through the far wall when one bullet fell on Mr Dowar's desk, hot but spent, just as he was about to sign a letter of complaint to the Station Commander about an altogether different matter. That one was immediately torn up, of course, and substituted by another in which he maintained we purposely tried to kill him and that he intended to raise the matter in The House at the earliest opportunity!

The AOC must be psychic, for he has just been on the telephone to say that 602 Squadron will be returning to Drem soon!

27th May The fine spell of weather did not last and it is raining cats and dogs again, in the middle of which three Ansons landed, when two of them came to grief in the mud. However one of them had brought in a new tail unit for Ian Ferguson's aircraft and Flight Sergeant Connors and his boys took no time to get it put on and have the Spitfire back on the line.

We don't like the sound of the news from France. The Germans have taken Amiens and Arras and our forces are having to fall back on the Channel ports. Furthermore we have a number of Fighter Command squadrons operating there and we gather that their losses have been high. In fact we are now wondering whether the lack of confirmation about our move to Drem may be tied up with this and that we are destined for a base nearer the scene of the action instead.

Four Tiger Moths came in to refuel during a let-up in the weather and we were surprised, and not a little delighted, to see they were being flown by girls of the Air Transport Auxiliary who were delivering them to Lossiemouth to go into temporary storage. Better still, I found that I knew two of the intrepid ladies, Mona Friedlander and Margaret Cunnison. In fact, I once went to Mona's rescue when she ran out of petrol while flying over Kent in 1938 and ran into a greenhouse during the subsequent forced landing. As I remember, it was a very warm day and Mona was wearing a rather brief pair of shorts and there was some problem about removing glass splinters from her shapely legs! However my previous acquaintanceship with Margaret was less erotic: We merely sat for our Commercial Pilot's Licences together.

So, after depositing the Moths at their appointed destination, the girls retured to Dyce in an Anson piloted by yet another member of the fair sex which naturally triggered off a jolly good party in the Mess afterwards. We saw the girls off yesterday morning only to find that Miss Cunnison had left behind her flying kit. However we were able to send it after her in another Anson which happened to be going their way. We noticed she had not forgotten her handbag, which is just as well, for doubtless that would be where the lipstick was kept!

We hear that Boulogne has now fallen, which means that our chaps are really up against it over there, and we were still weighing up our chances of being called on to help on the Continent when the AOC turned up unexpectedly to confirm our move to Drem. As things would have it, I was scrambled in the middle of the AOC's visit to investigate a sound plot off Findhorn, but it turned out to be nothing more menacing than a motor boat chugging along with a blown gasket!

I took our little teleprinter WAAF for a whirl round in a Tiger Moth as a sort of parting gesture, which she says she enjoyed although it was her first flight. There is little doubt that she has blossomed out under 602's tutelage!

28th May I kept myself off the flying programme yesterday to help with the packing up. However, Paul, Harry and Glyn carried out patrols over the Moray Firth without seeing anything of interest, and all the plots turned out to be friendly. We also got a confirmatory signal from Group about our pending move, in which it was emphasised that we had to ensure that a defensive posture was maintained throughout, so I brought Yellow Section to Drem on its own and reached there in time for breakfast. Dunlop arrived from Montrose with Red Section soon after.

Drem was looking strangely deserted, as 603 had already gone and one flight of 264 Squadron had also pushed off to the South, leaving their other flight flapping around awaiting our arrival. Now, they have gone too. Having breakfasted and cleaned up, I paid a courtesy visit to the Station Commander, who wilted visibly when he realised it was 602 Squadron which was returning, but he detailed the dispersals for our use and I checked them out before bringing Yellow Section back on the state to await the rest of the squadron. Donald Jack came in with Blue Section in the early evening whilst Archie brought up the rear with Green Section, who turned up at a quarter to midnight, thus completing our first unit move in darkness!

The broadcast news is bad. King Leopold of Belgium has thrown in the towel and the Germans thus have a clear route to Dunkirk, where the BEF is concentrating. It appears that our fellows are now carrying the main weight of the fighting on their shoulders.

31st May It is great to be back at Drem, for it has a happy atmosphere about it. Besides we will have our own second line servicing with us again, for these boys did not accompany us to Dyce and we have had to fly our aircraft back and forth whenever they required anything done to them. So, as Q has been surging a bit on take-off, I put her into the hangar straightaway. In any case, we are due to have armour plating fitted behind the pilots' seats, so both jobs can be attended to at the same time.

I nipped down to Gullane to call on Claire in the afternoon and found Bobbie Farquhar was staying with her. News of Douglas is good and he is enjoying his new job at Martlesham Heath. As Bobbie is only staying until tomorrow, Claire suggested that Margaret might come through and share the cottage with her for a spell. I am glad to say the suggestion met with unqualified approval when I rang Margaret that evening.

605 Squadron arrived on Thursday afternoon to rest and reform after a gruelling spell operating from airfields in France. They have lost nine aircraft and four pilots during the past six days and it looks as if Walter Churchill, the CO, will have a hard job ahead. However, these lads from Warwickshire are made of stern stuff and doubtless he will have them fighting fit in no time at all.

Paul and I spent this afternoon flogging a Tiger Moth round the area looking for possible emergency landing fields, but there seems to be a dearth of them. The only two which appealed to us are probably too far away, as one is near Berwick-on-Tweed whilst the other lies not far from Eyemouth.

Margaret has reacted quickly to Claire's kind invitation and took up residence in Hillview Cottage this evening.

June

4th June 'Disperse your aircraft. Spread them far and wide.' That's the universal cry these days, for we gather that a lot of fighters have been lost on the ground in France through neglect of this obvious precaution. Nevertheless it makes for much extra work, for our resources of ground servicing equipment are limited and will not go round all the aircraft at the same time, and therefore requires servicing personnel to drag heavy pieces of equipment from aeroplane to aeroplane, often over muddy and uneven ground. However, it is indeed a wise precaution and one which has been exercising us for long enough. So our thoughts once more turned to Macmerry.

George and I therefore got out the Magister and flew over to have a look at the place again and were glad to find the extension had been completed and all that was now required to make the place operable was to have the grass cut. In fact, some of it had grown so long that it reached to the top of the mainplane, and we must have looked more like a threshing machine than an aeroplane as we taxied towards the clubhouse building. However we reckoned it would do and, after arranging with the local Works and Bricks chap to have the field cut, George and I returned to Drem to work out a proper dispersal plan.

Someone has had the bright idea of fixing rear view mirrors to the Spitfires which should prevent us from getting cricks in our necks in the course of a dog fight. They will be a definite boon, but it makes one wonder what they will come up with next. Traffic indicators perhaps!

Having sat at readiness throughout Saturday and Sunday without being scrambled once, I went down to the cottage at eleven o'clock to find the AOC there. I was immediately told by him to return to the airfield as he had just had word that 602 Squadron was to leave for Northolt this afternoon! Apparently we were required to reinforce the air patrols covering the withdrawal of our forces from Dunkirk.

George had already got the message before I reached the Flight office and there was a hell of a flap going on as everything was packed up again and loaded on to the two Bombay transport aircraft which had flown in to take our essential equipment south. However, Group told us to hang on at Drem for the time being and that the Controller would tell us when to start moving. Thus we hung around the crew room throughout a nail-biting afternoon, during which some 605 boys looked in and tried to scare the daylights out of us with tales of the terrifying conditions over the Channel, at the end of which Group rang again to tell us that our move had been cancelled! I wish I had taken count of the number of visits that had been made to the loo during these few hours!

Finally made it to the cottage where I heard Winston Churchill announcing on the wireless that the evacuation of our troops from Dunkirk had been successfully completed. That was doubtless why our move was cancelled, but it nevertheless makes one wonder what comes next.

7th June We live in a strange climate, for we were wrapped up against the cold and wet only two weeks ago, whereas now the temperature was in the high sixties by eight o'clock this morning and was still rising. Long may it continue.

And strange things are happening on the ground too, for Charles Keary and George were both bidden to attend a Court Martial at Turnhouse the other day when I found myself standing in as the acting Station Commander! Imagine that! However, I did not fancy sitting at Charles Keary's desk all day, so gave Station Headquarters a miss and left word where I could be found if the need arose. As it happened, whoever was being tried at Turnhouse pleaded guilty and Charles and George were back on the station before the night state came on.

The weather was too good to miss so I put myself on the night state and took off on a practice trip around midnight. The night was beautifully clear and I was cruising over Lanarkshire at 32,000 feet, admiring the view, when I was suddenly aware of another Spitfire formating alongside me. It turned out to be Paul who had been scrambled to investigate an unidentified plot! Fool that I am, I had forgotten to let Ops know where I was. At least it is comforting to know the system still works, although a certain Flight Lieutenant has made himself somewhat unpopular in proving it!

George laid on a practice refuelling exercise at Tranent on Thursday when the object was to find out how long it would take to move a bowser and a fire tender over there in the event of us having to use the field. We took off with Green Section and circled over Tranent awaiting the arrival of the refuelling party, as we could not land until the fire services were in position. However, the inevitable happened and the ground party got hopelessly lost on the three mile stretch between the two airfields so that, by the time they eventually sorted themselves out, we really needed refuelling when we got in! But we found Tranent in a dreadful state and so bumpy that we were nearly rattled to bits when coming into land. I have recommended to George that we do not use the place except for a dire emergency.

A dense mist, known locally as a haar, has now rolled in and I have cancelled our air firing practice at Acklington laid on for tomorrow, for I have known it to hang about for days on end. Besides, Group is showing a spark of humanity and is allowing up to ten per cent of the fellows to go on leave as from today. George, being first in the queue, has therefore pushed off to inspect his rhubarb farm in Renfrewshire.

10th June As I thought, the mist persisted solidly throughout the last two days, but lifted sufficiently last night for us to lay on some night flying practice. However it started to form again while Red Section were up on patrol and the visibility was very poor by the time they rejoined the circuit. Although Dunlop got down all right, poor Hector had a particularly difficult landing, and after several abortive attempts to get down, finally arrived like a drunken hen when he broke a landing flap and wing tip and bent one of the oleo legs. However the maintenance boys excelled themselves and had the aircraft repaired and back on the line within four hours.

It is clear today and the weather has once more donned its summer garb. It was even quite comfortable flying at 20,000 feet in shirt sleeves with the hood open, which I found when patrolling Bell Rock this afternoon. However, I was somewhat embarrassed on returning to find Boom Trenchard at the dispersal, although he raised no objection to my rather unorthodox choice of flying gear. In fact, The Grand Old Man was in terrific form and, in no time at all, had us all firmly believing that the German Air Force was made up of nothing but a bunch of cissies! I always feel it is a privilege to talk to him, for he somehow symbolises all that is best in the Royal Air Force. There he was, wearing an old pattern uniform with turn--up trousers, no scrambled egg on his service cap, still carrying his white walking stick and holding his audience with every word he uttered. He had us in fits of laughter with his reminiscences and is obviously delighted to be in the House of Lords where, he told us, there are some six or seven Admirals and two or three Field Marshals to contend with, but that he felt in no way outnumbered even when they ganged up against him! I can well believe it, for he is indeed a very great man.

Birdie Saul was also present and I returned to the cottage with him after our distinguished visitor had left. It was so warm that we even persuaded the girls to come for a swim.

I should be across at Macmerry with B Flight tonight, but the AOC has given me dispensation and I am staying at the cottage instead.

The Italians have just declared war on the Allies. Isn't it just like them! They are nothing but a flock of vultures merely hanging about for the pickings.

14th June We had a rare treat on Tuesday when the Station dance band came to dispersal to play for the lads. It was an excellent orchestra made up from a number of ordinary airmen on the station who have had previous experience in the game. I was not over-surprised at the professional performance they put on after discovering that two of its members had once played with Ambrose's orchestra in the Mayfair, whilst a third had played alongside Jack Jackson in the Dorchester.

No patrols were called for during the day and I took B Flight to Macmerry last night to find out for myself what it was like. As a matter of fact it was dashed comfortable, equipped as it was with beds and sheets, and we also had a go at using the portable Primus cooker to prepare something for our supper. However, poor old Harry had an unfortunate encounter with some boiling fat when one of the sausages he was frying suddenly spat at him and caught him painfully unawares! Alas, he had stripped down to his underpants on account of the heat and failed to appreciate the joke when it hit him amidships!

However Alastair Grant saved the day, or I should say the night, when he drove over with a bottle of champagne with which to celebrate his recent engagement. Unfortunately we did not see very much of it as Harry claimed the lion's share to assuage his hurt feelings! There is also a Company of Dragoons at Macmerry doing guard duty and they kept us awake most of the night with their clumping big tackety boots. I can never understand why soldiers have to make so much noise when they walk about. They seem to love stamping their feet and shouting at one another!

We think French resistance is beginning to crumble, for the Germans are fast approaching Paris and we hear that the French government has done a bunk to somewhere less vulnerable. Winston Churchill is doing his best to boost their morale and has even offered France joint citizenship with the UK to keep them in the war, but we are beginning to realise now that we may have to go it alone soon. The prospect is a daunting one.

Having done the dawn patrol on the way back from Macmerry this morning we landed to find that the squadron had been released from operations for the rest of the day, so we used the opportunity

aken at Drem in February 940—note the snow on the round.

n convoy patrol, February 940.

eaving Harwell, September 940.

Archie McKellar.

Blessing ceremony, June 1940 at Drem. S
Harry Lauder with Padre Sutherland.

Blessing the Spitfire and Hurricane at Drem, June 1940.

to try out some new combat formations. Hitherto we have flown in four sections with three aircraft in each. However, as a result of our experiment, we now find the whole thing becomes more manoeuvrable when the section strength is converted to two and two, as it were. In other words, The Squadron will now consist of three sections of four Spitfires instead of the old set up with four sections of three. At any rate we intend to give it a whirl.

In spite of the gravity of affairs elsewhere, all was serene at the cottage, where I found Margaret and Claire gossipping like a pair of old sweetywives. We celebrated the news of the fall of Paris by opening a bottle of champagne and going for a midnight bathe!

18th June Harry Moody and Pay Lyall have received their Commissions and we are all delighted to see them in the Mess. It is just as well things are quiet in the Scottish Sector for the worthy lads were not slow in ensuring we all helped to celebrate their new-found status. Fortunately even the convoys were taking a day off!

My turn has come to take leave, so I took Margaret to the West for a few days. Having spent Sunday night with my parents, we went on to Prestwick the following day and were astounded at the changes which were taking place there. The north side of the airfield appeared to be in the hands of workmen who were in the course of putting up a huge building and a hangar to match. It appears that David MacIntyre has persuaded his company, Scottish Aviation Ltd, to purchase the building which housed the Palace of Engineering at the 1938 Commonwealth Exhibition in Bellahouston Park, and is having it re-erected at Prestwick as a factory in which he intends to build new aircraft. It certainly sounds an ambitious project, and I hope it will succeed.

However, on the Navigation School side, two of the men have managed to write off the largest of the three Fokker trainers when they had an argument during take-off about which of them was controlling the throttles in this strange aeroplane. The only thing that took off in the end was a brood of hens as the Fokker ignominiously ploughed its way through a chicken run at the far corner of the field! Thankfully, none of the twenty or so people on board were hurt, although I gather the pilot's pride is decidedly so!

Having spent an enjoyable night with many old friends in the Orangefield, we pressed on to visit an uncle and aunt at Uplawmoor where we found that both Jean and Archie have become members of the local ARP outfit, of which they are immensely proud. Naturally, I had to be shown around and be introduced to the rest of the Uplawmoor worthies, whom I found to be embarrassingly conscientious in their approach to the job. For instance, none go anywhere without their gas masks and tin hats, except Jean that is, for she maintains the helmet gives her a headache and turns up for duty wearing a frilly tea cosy instead! It's not a bad alternative when one thinks about it, although I think we would have considerable difficulty persuading the Air Ministry to adopt the fashion!

As it so happened, Uplawmoor was in the grip of a drought and the only water came from a standpipe erected at the far end of the village so, being the dutiful nephew, I made no fewer than three trips to the standpipe to bring back pails of water. I was glad I was only staying for the one night!

The news now speaks of France seeking an Armistice with Germany which, if true, will leave Britain in a damnably exposed position. Maybe the Yanks will pitch in now.

21st June We called to see Margaret's sister on our way through Glasgow and found her in a bit of a state, as her husband Jim has been called up for the Army, which makes me wonder what will become of the Alvis! Claire was also in a state by the time we got back to Gullane, for the place has apparently been buzzing with rumours of invasion and another dear soul has been insisting that she saw Germans landing, this time in Aberlady Bay. A bad case of the willies, I fear!

However Drem is certainly taking life more seriously and a curfew has been imposed nightly from ten thirty. Furthermore, the sentries now have orders not to let anyone in or out of the camp without receiving the correct password. Things are happening outside the camp too, and large numbers of Royal Engineers and civilian contractors are swarming over the beaches, erecting jagged posts and putting up concrete pill boxes all along the foreshore.

They say they are to prevent gliders from landing but I fear they will also prevent any further thoughts of going midnight bathing!

Five new pilots arrived for the Squadron today – Pilot Officer Rose and Sergeants Sprague, Proctor, Elcome and Whipps – none of whom have been given previous operational training. Also Archie McKellar has been promoted to Flight Lieutenant and posted as a Flight Commander in 605 Squadron. So we have a training job ahead of us. However, Birdie Saul is at the cottage this evening and tells me he is arranging for his ADC, Mickey Mount, to join us and that he will be taking Muspratt-Williams to replace him. We will be sorry to lose Spratt but delighted to have Mickey, who is going to have a conversion course on Spitfires before joining us.

Business suddenly became brisk earlier today, but we believe it was due more to the now fashionable complaint of jitteryness than to any upsurge of enemy interest. At all events, we carried out eleven patrols with damn all to show for them.

24th June The haar rolled in again a couple of days ago and put flying out of the question. It was frustrating too, because we heard the sound of a Hun reconnaissance aircraft overhead and could do nothing about it. However the local anti-aircraft boys chucked a few rounds in its general direction and Jerry turned back the way he had come. I shouldn't think he could see anything either.

In its usual unpredictable fashion the mist cleared as suddenly as it had rolled in and I was able to fly to Turnhouse to meet George Denholm, the CO of 603 Squadron. As we have such a heavy training programme ahead of us, I was anxious to be relieved of as much of the operational load as possible for the next week or so, and George was most co-operative and agreed we should co-ordinate our readiness states for the time being. Besides there is no point in both squadrons keeping chaps at readiness unnecessarily. I was pleased to find Findlay getting on with the training programme when I got back and the circuit at Drem seemed to be full of Fun Fair take-offs as the new lads experienced the idiosyncracies of the undercarriage lever for the first time. They will soon get the better of the whoopsy motion!

News from the other side of The Channel is bleak, for the French

have signed an Armistice with Germany and are now negotiating a
further one with Italy. Apparently France is to be allowed to keep a
puppet government at Vichy to run the southern part of the country
whilst the Germans take complete control of the northern portion.
It is sad to see a once proud nation go under like this. I wonder
what went wrong.

Spent Sunday at the cottage. Birdie was also there this week end
and was the bearer of interesting news. Charles Keary is to be
replaced as Station Commander at Drem by Dick Atcherley and
the mind boggles at the thought, for I cannot think of two people
who are less alike. It will be a complete metamorphosis. Whereas
Charles is pedantic, a strict disciplinarian, a conformist and
remote, Batchy is one of the boys. A hero of the successful
Schneider Trophy team of the mid thirties, a brilliant pilot, a most
approachable man and one with a legendary reputation for knock-
ing off policemen's helmets! It should make an interesting change.

Mickey and Spratt were also at the cottage and we put them to
work helping to build an air raid shelter at the end of the garden.
Birdie and I had decided to reinforce an old disused pigsty with
sandbags and corrugated metal sheeting and have put in it a bed,
tinned food, bottles of water and a hurricane lamp, and have
threatened the girls with dire penalties if they don't go into it as
soon as the sirens sound. Birdie says he will even cut off their supply of gin if they don't comply!

A bit of bad news from the other side of the airfield. Barry
Goodwin of 605 Squadron has just spun in near Dunbar and has
been killed instantly. What a pity, after surviving the rigours of
Dunkirk.

26th June Have spent the past two days concentrating on training
sessions with some of the new pilots who, I am pleased to report,
are coming along famously. I had both Sergeants Sprague and
Proctor up with me on formation practice and they are managing to
keep up with their leader, even during the more violent manoeuvres
one encounters in combat. I also let Harry Moody go in front for a
while, for there is an art in leading a formation as well as in just
following it.

Had been hoping to spend last night in the cottage, but it was not to be, and I was recalled to the Flight in the middle of supper. Apparently Jerry was being troublesome and bombs were reported falling on Lanarkshire and on the outskirts of Edinburgh as well.

I was ordered off round about midnight and vectored westwards in the direction of Edinburgh. As I climbed to the designated height I could see a number of searchlights weaving a pattern in the sky, and occasional flashes from ack-ack shells bursting in the far distance. Suddenly three beams converged, when I noticed an aircraft caught in their apex. Needless to say, I was flabbergasted to see it was a Heinkel. Tallyho! Switching on the reflector gunsight and the firing safety ring, I opened the throttle and sped to the target which was now clearly visible ahead of me. To be truthful, my mind was by now in such a whirl of excitement that I forgot to slow down, and jolly nearly collided with my target, and had to pull sharply to one side at the last moment without firing a shot. Fortunately the searchlight boys knew their stuff and held the Heinkel in their beams while I tried to sort myself out. A rather bad start, I fear! However, I managed to line up properly next time and let go with the eight Brownings when the Spitfire shuddered violently under their recoil. The Heinkel disappeared from sight.

'Gosh,' I thought, 'I've downed it first go!'

Not me! My windscreen was only covered in oil from one of the target's engines, which made me think I must have hit it at least. So I flew alongside and saw one of its engines was on fire leaving a thick pall of black smoke streaming behind. Bits flew off the Heinkel on my second attack, when I realised he was going down, for a glance at the altimeter showed we were already below one thousand feet. However, I had no idea where we were, for apart from the light from the searchlights, the night was pitch dark and the glare from the beams had destroyed what little night vision would have been possible in the circumstances.

The pilot of the Heinkel suddenly switched on his landing light and dipped below the searchlight beams, when I realised for the first time that we were over the sea and not far from the town of Dunbar. The Hun was obviously preparing to ditch and I was fascinated to watch the huge splash as he hit the water and the glow from the landing light grow fainter as it slowly disappeared beneath the waves.

I immediately climbed to 2000 feet and pulled off the colours of the day, a double red Very light as I remember, to mark the spot where I had watched the Jerry plane go down and returned to Drem, hoping that someone had seen it going down and would send a boat to search for survivors.

Corporal Burnett, my rigger, was first to greet me as I taxied in, and pressed a mug of steaming hot cocoa into my hand before I had even got out of the cockpit. Thereafter I found the crew room buzzing with excitement when I entered, for apparently I had delivered the coup de grace directly over Drem and the lads had had a grandstand view of the action. It naturally crossed my mind that Margaret and Claire would also have been able to watch it.

The Intelligence Officer seemed to take a devil of a long time to fill out his report although, in fairness to him, the poor fellow had been hauled from his bed at two in the morning, and may therefore be excused. Also there was a further hold up when the police from Dunbar rang up to tell us that three of the German crew had been picked up and brought ashore in the local lifeboat. They added that the pilot was a cocky little blighter of eighteen years of age who took a delight in spitting on a nurse who was trying to attend to his superficial injuries. So it was some hours before I was able to ring through to the cottage, only to find that neither Claire nor Margaret had seen anything of the performance. They had taken our strictures to heart and went to the shelter as soon as the sirens sounded! Doubtless they had their supply of gin in mind!

28th June Was trying to catch up on lost sleep after the exertions of the previous night, when I received a summons to report to the Station Commander's office immediately.

It was obvious, as soon as I entered, that something had gone wrong, for Batchy was using all his considerable charm to placate two rather wearisome Army officers who had driven from Edinburgh to see him and who were asking what the devil we thought we were playing at firing off two red Very lights over Dunbar in the middle of the night!

What they knew, but had evidently forgotten to tell us, was that a double red light to the Army meant that an invasion was imminent. So the poor soldiery had been turned out to a man and stood by from Fife to The Borders awaiting the attack which never came! We could only say we were sorry, but would they please not be so secretive about their signals in future. At all events, I am glad to report that our visitors recovered their sense of humour after Batchy and I had taken them for a noggin in the Officers' Mess.

I again found myself on state last night and was again scrambled at 11.30 towards the capital city. As I was climbing through 18,000 feet I caught a fleeting glance of another He 111 streaking past my starboard wingtip, but going in the opposite direction. The blighter must have spotted me for he shoved his nose down and, by the time I had swung round in pursuit, he had been swallowed up in the darkness and was out of sight. However, I followed his plot far out to sea and only gave up the chase when my fuel began to run low. It was a pity, for it would have been nice to have clobbered two bandits in so many nights.

Drem was under Red Alert when I rejoined the circuit and all the lights had been doused. However, Paul and Ian managed to get three paraffin flares going in time to let me down before the last of the petrol ran out, but it was not an easy landing, as long streaks of flame stream back from the exhaust stubs when one closes the throttles of a Spitfire and they effectively obscure the flarepath when approaching at night. Of course, the effect was magnified when I had only the three flares on which to line up and, indeed, I was only able to come in at all by making the approach at right angles, so as to keep the lights in sight over the edge of the cockpit combing, before turning in at the last moment and doing the rest from memory. However Batchy was at the dispersal when I landed and promised to turn his inventive mind to find a solution to the problem. Just give him time, he says.

At the moment, however, Batchy is more concerned about dispersing the aircraft and, for the second morning running, I had my hard earned sleep disturbed by the Station Commander's call to attend at his office at once. Walter Churchill was already there when I arrived and I guessed from his wry smile that we were in for a drubbing of some sort. And we were not kept waiting for it either!

'Useless! Ruddy useless! Worse than useless, in fact!' when we knew that Batchy was referring to our past efforts to spread our aircraft about the airfield. 'We'll go and find something better right away!'

So saying, he summoned his staff car, once the pride and joy of Charles Keary, no longer shiny blue but now liberally bedaubed with blobs of green and buff coloured camouflage paint, and whisked Walter and me off on a whirlwind tour of East Lothian at the end of which we were no better off than we had been before! Even Batchy agreed that Tranent in its present state was too rough, although that does not mean that he will not commandeer half the local council's work force to have it levelled off. He's that sort of chap. Am writing this in the cottage and hoping for a peaceful night for a change. But Jerry is obviously keeping the pressure on us for I have already heard two Spitfires taking off. However, A Flight is doing the state tonight and I am sure Dunlop and Donald are more than capable of keeping them at bay!

30th June The month ended peacefully and I have only had to do one patrol during the past three days, and it was over the Firth of Forth, when I took Sergeant Sprague on his first operational sortie. He kept station well and tucked himself in close when required. It should not take long to get him checked out at this rate. At all events, the patrol ended up in an ogo-pogo whilst we chased our own plots between North Berwick and Crail, but Sprague said he thoroughly enjoyed the trip. Such is the enthusiasm of inexperience!

The AOC and Marcus are both here this week end and they were invited with the rest of us, by the South Wales Borderers, to their cocktail party in Bisset's Hotel. Marcus is taking time off from trying to lick his squadron into shape after taking a hammering over France earlier in the month. Birdie and I played golf this morning, thinking it would help to clear our heads after the Army's hospitality, but the truth of the matter is that we had to pack it in after seven holes as we had lost all our golf balls by then!

July

1st July Led two sorties this morning, when one at least should have
shown a dividend. Regretfully I have to report we failed to take advantage of the opportunities offered. Control put us on to a plot on
the first sortie, but it turned out to be a stern chase and our target
showed us a clean pair of heels. We had to turn back when we were
nearly seventy miles out to sea because the weather was atrocious
out there, with a solid wall of cloud stretching from sea level to
goodness knows what height, for we were still in the clag at 25,000
feet. However, just as Paul and I were sitting down to lunch, we
were called to readiness – I am beginning to think the Hun does
this purposely just to annoy us! – and were scrambled over Dunbar
where the cloud cover was still mainly thick, but with broken-
patches in places.

As we approached the town we caught sight of a Ju 88 nipping
out of one billowy cloud and into another, and heading for Dunbar.
However, he must have spotted us too, for the crew jettisoned their
bombs about a mile short of the target and turned for home. A cat
and mouse chase ensued while the Junkers dodged from cloud to
cloud and Paul actually managed to get in a burst from a beam
position before he scudded into another bit of cover. We saw him
only once again when he seemed to be still going well! Paul claims

he saw smoke coming from one of the Ju's engines but I suspect it was more likely caused by Jerry bending his throttles wide open as he fled for home. At any rate, Intelligence are not prepared to credit us with anything, although I have little doubt that we gave him a hell of a fright! It makes me wonder whether we should not introduce another category to the accepted three forms of claims – 'Destroyed', 'Probably Destroyed', and 'Damaged'. It could be designated 'Scared Fartless'!

3rd July Air Chief Marshal Ludlow-Hewitt, The Inspector General of the RAF, visited us on Tuesday and was interested to hear about our brush with the Ju 88. It is a pity it had not ended more successfully. However, he invited me to accompany him to Turnhouse, but we had no sooner got there when a flap started in the Operations Room, as a Dornier 17 had apparently just sneaked in low over Drem and had straafed the field on the way past. In fact, it just missed hitting Yellow Section as it was taking off on a belated scramble order and made off before Findlay and his boys could get after it. The Dornier had flown in under the RDF cover which certainly underlines the need for dispersing the aircraft properly when they are parked on the ground.

I borrowed a Tiger Moth to get back to Drem quickly and counted five large bomb craters between Dalkeith and North Berwick all, fortunately, in open fields. In fact, the only creatures who appeared to be unduly disturbed were a number of cows which I saw looking disconsolately at the destruction of their pasture! As expected, Batchy was hopping mad that the Dornier had got away.

I took the flight to Macmerry last night where Batchy has us dispersed, as well as at Drem. No longer do we enjoy the comfort of the clubhouse building to offset the tedium of parking over there. No, we are scattered round the perimeter, sleeping rough under canvas. Of course, it rained cats and dogs all night and the blasted tents were leaking like sieves. But otherwise we had an undisturbed night!

Was scrambled to patrol over Arbroath this afternoon at Angels 20 and ran into a Dornier 17 on the way up. It was darting in and out of clouds at 14,000 feet. I managed to get in a short burst before he reached cloud cover, but that was all I saw of him. The only consolation I could draw from the brief engagement was that the Jerry rear gunner also fired at me and missed! At all events, neither of us succeeded in doing any harm to the other, but I must really take a grip on myself and stop becoming so excited when this sort of thing crops up unexpectedly. That's the second time I have reacted in this way and there is really no excuse for it. Mind you, things do happen quickly, particularly when one meets the enemy head on, as I did on this occasion, as the closing speed of the two aircraft must be in the region of 600 m.p.h. at least. However, both Ops and I lost contact with this one, so can only assume he stuffed his nose down and beat it back home at sea level.

7th July Ops has warned us that the Germans are stepping up their efforts, particularly against coastal shipping, and as we have several convoys passing through our area, the Flights are now taking turn about of keeping a section at stand-by. Also everyone is now confined to camp which, although aggravating from a domestic point of view, at least saves the bother of having to remember the correct password of the day!

Jerry must have got wind of our special precautions and taken fright, for he never showed up! We maintained tne stand-by posture for three days and nights during which I only did one sortie, and that was over North Berwick where I scoured the sky above and below the clouds without seeing anything more exciting than a small boy flying his kite from the harbour wall.

We have been released from our confinement this evening when I took the girls to Haddington to see Charles Boyer and Irene Dunne in *When Tomorrow Comes*. I thought it was a ghastly picture, but Margaret and Claire loved it and wept copiously throughout! However Findlay and Hector had been busy while I was off the station. They shot a Ju 88 into the sea near May Island.

9th July Tiredness is beginning to catch up with me, for I overslept this morning and only awakened when a Spitfire took off low over the cottage at ten o'clock. Fortunately I was not due to go on the state until midday. As it was, Paul and I were just in the midst of climbing into our flying gear when we were scrambled to go after a high flying plot approaching Fife. The Controller told us we were closing on the target, but it was not until we cleared the tops of the cumulus at 20,000 feet that Paul saw a Heinkel 111 nipping in and out of their tops quite near us, but making for home and not towards Scotland, as we had been told.

We had to stalk our quarry for some time, as he kept jinking from one cloud to another and we never knew where he was going to appear next. However we eventually got it right and both of us were able to let him have a co-ordinated burst from both quarters when its starboard engine burst into flames and the aircraft dived smartly into the nearest cloud. There was a considerable amount of return fire from the Heinkel but neither Paul nor I were hit. Unhappily we were unable to make further contact with it to deliver a coup de grace. It was a long drag back to Drem but at least we are being allowed a 'Probable' for the action. Apparently a few bombs had been dropped at Crail, without doing any damage, while we had been airborne and Drem itself had been under Red Alert. I later heard that the girls had been in their shelter!

George Pinkerton has gone on leave again, leaving me to run the Squadron, so I used the privilege to sneak a night off at the cottage. Serves me right for doing so, for I had no sooner got there when A Flight was ordered off and intercepted a couple of Ju 88's two miles off the coast. Dunlop shot one down whilst Donald put a lot of bullets into the other, although we don't yet know its ultimate fate. I naturally felt rather sheepish when I heard about it, for it is hardly the done thing for the acting Squadron Commander to be found washing a dog in the garden while his colleagues are beating the daylights out of the enemy only a few miles away! I have made a mental note to stay nearer the sharp end in future!

11th July Batchy sent for Walter and me yesterday morning to tell us about his latest brainwave. He had been exercising his mind, he said, about the ever pressing problem of dispersing the aircraft out of sight of marauding aircraft, and had come to the conclusion that the place to put them was in the middle of the wood which lies close to the southern boundary of the airfield. We would scoop out places for aircraft standings after which no one would guess there were any aeroplanes there at all! 'We'll start right now!' he said.

The rain was coming down in buckets, so Walter and I put on our wellies and raincoats and set off to reconnoitre the wood with Batchy. We took two airmen with us, each carrying a large pot of white paint and a paint brush, and crashed our way through the sodden undergrowth with everything above us pouring cascades of water on top of us. Nothing daunted, we set to work, marking with a dash of paint those trees and large shrubs which would have to be moved to allow access, but it was dank, dark and dismal in that wretched wood and all four of us were exhausted when we eventually emerged from it. Not so Batchy, who remained as bright and breezy as ever and who clearly regarded his scheme as good as done! In any case, it was not for the likes of us to argue the toss with our Station Commander, although in truth, Walter and I wondered what we had been let in for!

Was well nigh pooped by the time I had dealt with the bumff in the Orderly Room. I do wish the boys would not bend so many aircraft, for every incident involving one of our Spitfires requires a report to be written on the circumstances by the Squadron Commander. I was glad to turn in early.

Walter and I were in the wood again first thing this morning without even the luxury of two airmen to carry the paints pots. The rain never let up either, and we had it running down our necks and the insides of our wellington boots. Goodness me, I have never come across a wood in which so many trees required to be painted! At any rate, our arms were aching when we packed it in late in the afternoon when I got a chance to look in at the Squadron office. There was a message waiting for me to say that the AOC was at the cottage and wanted to see me as soon as I was free. Naturally I took it to be urgent and went there without stopping to tidy up, all the time wondering what I could have done wrong!

However Birdie was most affable and began by introducing me to his brother whom he had not seen for years and who had just arrived unexpectedly from Canada. Then he asked me how was the CO of 602 Squadron, which I thought was strange, as he himself had signed George's leave warrant only a few days previously. I

reminded him of this, adding that as far as I knew, George was
well.

'If the CO is on leave, then he has gone off without my permission,' he countered.

Needless to say I was rather taken aback by this turn in the conversation and tried to remonstrate on my CO's behalf, when the
AOC interrupted with a 'Don't get into a tizzy, Sandy. What I am
telling you is that I am having you appointed CO of the squadron
as from tomorrow!'

Talk about having the wind knocked out of ones sails – you could
have knocked me down with a feather, if you will pardon the mixed
metaphor!

Today is Claire and Birdie's fourth wedding anniversary:
Findlay's kill the other night had brought 13 Group's total of victories up to the fifty mark: The unexpected return from Canada of
the prodigal brother: Add to these my own unexpected elevation,
and we had the ingredients for a jolly good celebration which Birdie
was not slow to exploit. He took us all to the De Guise for a slap-up
dinner during which, I must confess, I was awfully conscious of the
white paint under my fingernails!

13th July Understandably, I awoke with a thick head yesterday
morning but, in spite of it, I was looking at the world through rose
coloured glasses and felt as if I was walking on air! Even the rain
had stopped as I approached the wood with a light step – indeed it
would be more correct to say that I approached it with an eager
step, as my new found status had given me a sense of proprietorship
which acted as a spur to get *my* Spitfires under cover as quickly as
possible! But the grass had not been growing under Batchy's feet
either and we found him already in the wood talking to a represen-
tative from the firm of contractors who were going to do the job,
deciding on the number of bulldozers to be used, how much back
filling would be required, and so on. In fact we find much of
Batchy's enthusiasm is beginning to rub off on us and that the
woodland project has become a matter of top priority for both
Walter and me.

Paul took Rose, Sprague and Phillips to Carlisle by train yesterday to collect four new Spitfires from the Maintenance Unit, which has now brought us up to strength in aircraft. This is a good situation with which to start my stewardship of the unit. Furthermore, all our new boys have been passed fit for daylight operations.

Having got Project Number One safely launched, Batchy has now turned his attention to the second, that of finding somewhere quiet where off-duty air crews can sleep undisturbed at nights. He has invoked help from the girls for this and spent several hours whisking them round the countryside in his staff car looking at houses, checking distances, and so forth. I called at the cottage last night and found Margaret and Claire looking thoroughly shattered, which made me remember that I had forgotten to warn them about Batchy's driving. It is, after all, an unusual experience for the uninitiated, as he only knows two speeds – flat out and stopped – and wastes no time between the two! Also he has another disconcerting theory that the faster he traverses a road crossing, the less time there is for the other fellow to hit him! I realised my omission as soon as I went into the house, for the girls don't normally drink doubles!

However a rather pleasant by-product came from the house hunting expeditions when the four of us were invited to dinner at Gilmerton House by one of his prospective victims, Sir David Kinloch. It is a beautiful country house and was high on Batchy's short list but, after the delightful and generous hospitality of our charming host and hostess, even Batchy was constrained to remove Gilmerton House from the list of possibles!

There was quite a bit of enemy activity last night when bombs were dropped on Greenock and Cardross. Why Cardross, I cannot think for there is nothing of military importance anywhere near there. The boys patrolled at frequent intervals throughout the period but were unable to make any interceptions. Fortunately the damage has been reported as being only slight.

We were down in the wood again today finishing off the tree-marking chore as the bulldozers are expected in early next week to start the clearance operation. Flight Sergeant Connors offered to lend a hand and manfully wielded his paint brush to such an extent that he ended up with more paint on himself than on the trees!

A signal came in this afternoon confirming my appointment as CO and also notifying my promotion to the rank of acting squadron leader. So, having lashed out on a champagne party in the Mess earlier in the evening, I am once again back at the cottage and suffering from a severe bout of heartburn!

17th July Two large bulldozers arrived on Tuesday and immediately got down to work, when large trees, small trees, large bushes and small bushes appeared to be disdainfully tossed aside as Batchy's scheme began to take shape. They were at least a hundred yards into the wood at the end of two hours work. The next job was to set down sites to be used as fuel dumps so, as the rain had started to come down, out came the wellies and raincoats again as Walter and I made our selections. However, as I have mentioned earlier, the dispersal scheme was not confined to Drem alone and Walter and I later flew over to Macmerry to repeat the performance there.

As they say in the case of women, a squadron commander's work is never done, and I had no sooner cleared away the office chores when Walter and I were whisked off to look at Hope House as Batchy reckoned it would make a suitable rest house for the off-duty aircrew. It certainly had everything we were looking for, being nicely tucked into the Lammermuir Hills. At all events we agreed it would do, so that is Project Number Two safely disposed of.

George Pinkerton was waiting for me when I got back, so we straightaway got down to the handing over formalities. I feel very sorry for George, for he did not have very long in the hot seat.

It appears the Germans are putting pressure on the chaps in the South and are concentrating on attacking convoys of ships passing through The Straits of Dover. They have also been making periodic attacks on the CH and CHL Stations dotted along the South Coast which could be serious, as we depend upon this RDF Chain for most of our early warning. However our boys are doing well and are giving a good account of themselves. We hear the Germans have also moved a number of heavy calibre guns on to the French coast and are firing them at passing shipping. Under these circumstances, it seems damned silly to be running ships at all in that area!

RAF Montrose was under air attack yesterday evening when a Master Trainer was damaged whilst taxying and a petrol dump received a direct hit. I gather there was one hell of a blaze, but that there were no casualties. We tried to send off Green Section in the middle of it to help out, but the weather beat us. Even the bulldozers are now bogged down!

19th July The weather had improved by this morning and we were able to get A Flight off to Dyce to reinforce the north in case the Luftwaffe should pay a return visit. At the same time, work recommenced on gouging out the centre of the wood where today we have had a busload of willing helpers from Fettes College lending a hand. Batchy had previously called on the Headmaster and had persuaded him that working in the woods would be a healthier occupation for the boys than poring over their Latin conjugations indoors. At all events, the lads have been working like beavers and the dispersal project is rapidly taking shape.

The AOC has been on the telephone and has given me permission to bring our two Command Reserve aeroplanes into the front line. I am relieved by this, for we are rather under strength at the moment, having A Flight away in the north. The new unit will be labelled Black Section. Supermarine's Chief Test Pilot, Geoffrey Quill, also flew in today with a new gadget for us to try out in the shape of a Spitfire fitted with a variable pitch airscrew instead of the usual two-speed model. I flew the aircraft this afternoon and liked it, for it gives one a very smooth ride compared with the one fitted with the old push and pull device. In the VP model the speed of the propeller remains constant and the desired pitch of its blades can be selected by merely opening and closing a lever mounted alongside the throttle, thereby sparing one from the often jerky transition from fine to coarse pitch. I think the lads will like it.

As the boys from Fettes had done so well, Batchy was anxious that all who wanted a flight should be given one. So we commandeered the serviceable aircraft from Station Flight and set to work getting them airborne. We got together a small flying circus comprising two Tiger Moths, two Harvard Trainers and a Fairey Battle, whilst Batchy augmented the force by borrowing a visiting

Blenheim in which he took the boys up four at a time. On one occasion I watched the Blenheim flashing across the airfield upside down at nought feet! Even after that experience the boys said they had enjoyed the flight, so obviously they teach them how to be diplomatic at Fettes College!

25th July Jerry is still concentrating his efforts on coastal shipping in the south with the result that, every time a convoy comes into our area, the blokes in Ops become so sensitive that I feel they would have us airborne if only a fly should walk across the plotting table! In fact, we are being sent off so often nowadays that one wonders why they don't go the whole hog and keep up a standing patrol instead!

Douglas Farquhar has come up for a few days' leave and I was able to show him the dispersal scheme in the wood, which is now coming along so well that we are able to put a Tiger Moth into it to show it off. I therefore flew Douglas over the site in another Moth this afternoon to let him see for himself how effective is the camouflage.

Unfortunately I had to leave our visitor to his own devices this evening as there was so much enemy air activity about. In fact, Harry Moody was up on his inaugural night patrol when a Ju 88 suddenly appeared from nowhere, streaked low across the airfield without firing at anything, and disappeared in the direction of Edinburgh without so much as by your leave. I immediately scrambled Ian Ferguson to go after it and informed Ops what I had done. The Controller was just as surprised as we had been, for he had nothing on his table to show that a hostile was in the area. Again an intruder had slipped in unnoticed below the RDF cover!

The raider got clean away after dropping some bombs on the outskirts of Edinburgh, one of which fell on a cemetery near Leith in which we had buried some of the German crews who had been shot down during the raid on the Firth of Forth last October. Indeed it was a strange quirk of fate that two of the grisly remains which were exposed as a result of this raid turned out to be those of Germans whom we had buried with full military honours only nine months before.

27th July. General Stumpff's boys must like Scotland, for they are frequent visitors to our shores these days. The General's squadrons are operating from captured airfields in Norway, part of Luftflotte Five – *Stumpff's Funf,* we call them – but although a few of them venture inland during the hours of darkness, they seldom come further than within landfall in their daylight operations. They do not seem to be showing the same aggressive spirit that they used to. At all events I am concentrating as much effort as possible into bringing up more pilots to night operational standard, and Batchy has promised to turn his attention towards the safety factors involved.

We have now set up two Q-sites of our own. I have mentioned these on a previous occasion in relation to operations near Scapa Flow, but I think a word of explanation would not go amiss here. Q-Sites are nothing but dummy flarepaths laid out on open ground far removed from any form of habitation, in the hope of fooling the enemy into believing they are airfields engaged in night flying operations. In fact, the Germans have already dropped many bombs on such decoys all over the country, but we have never had one near Drem until now. So I took the MT fellows who have been given the job of laying and lighting up the flares, to see the areas on the nearby moors where they are to operate, in the sincere hope that they won't mislead our own pilots instead!

McDowall and I were both patrolling last night, when Mac had a crack at a Heinkel which had been momentarily illuminated by a searchlight over Dunbar. He claims to have registered hits on the intruder, but it had taken refuge in cloud and he had not been able to follow it down. I had latched on to another about the same time, but some distance off the coast of Fife. This one immediately jettisoned its bombs and dived to sea level when I lost sight of it in the darkness. I was flying Q with its newly fitted VP airscrew on this trip and it worked a treat.

I am just off to bed now, for I feel very weary.

28th July The Jerries are over every night now, mostly engaged in laying mines along the convoy routes, but they are difficult to catch, as they have obviously cottoned on to the shortcomings of our warning system and fly in at low level to avoid early detection. And the mines are taking their toll too, for only the other day I saw the *Royal Archer* run into one of them off St. Abb's Head while escorting the convoy she was in, and quickly go under with half her bows blown away.

However, we are now able to put up standing patrols at night which can fly along clearly defined tracks, thanks to our friends in the Searchlights who have agreed to mark certain positions with different coloured beams. For instance, we now know that a vertical green beam shines from Haddington, a red one from Dunbar and a mauve coloured beam comes from Loanhead, and so on. Our chaps only have to fly a patrol line between two designated colours to know exactly where they are. The searchlight boys also help by laying a horizontal beam pointing towards Drem as an additional aid to navigation. It has been a great boon, especially for the new boys, and we are most grateful to them for their co-operation.

Having got the night state teed up at Drem and the off-duty chaps ready to go over to Macmerry, I went down to the cottage for my evening meal but, as seems to be my accustomed fate these days, had to dash off in the middle of it to drive to Macmerry when one of our Spitfires came to grief there. Nigel Rose had hit a marker post coming in to land and it had ripped open the parachute flare tube and set off the pyrotechnic inside. A large hole has been burned in the underside of the fuselage which, of course, will mean more paper work for the Squadron Commander! I was annoyed at missing my evening at the cottage for Rachael Willoughby de Broke had been there and I was keen to find out if she knew what had really gone wrong in Belgium. Rachael and John had been friendly with King Leopold in earlier days and had probably kept in touch with him.

And now it is Sunday. The Day of Rest. You're kidding! Not while Wing Commander Atcherley is Station Commander! No indeed. It is the churchmen's day and Batchy has decided they needed a boost by arranging a swep-up church parade during which a Spitfire from 602 Squadron and a Hurricane from 605 Squadron were to be given the once-over by the men of God. A sort of Blessing Ceremony.

We got N properly buffed up, Walter wheeled out his cleanest

Hurricane, chairs were laid out for the visiting dignitaries, amongst whom were the AOC, wives, local friends, Sir Harry Lauder and his niece Greta, and everyone sat down as if attending an orchestral concert, whilst Padre Sutherland's lusty voice did its stentorian stuff once more. The rain kept off and the two aircraft were duly annointed, after which Sir Harry performed in one of the hangars which had been cleaned out for the occasion. But not before this grand old comedian had had his high tea without which, Greta told us, he would never go on. At all events, it was a masterly performance and the old maestro has lost none of his verve and can still belt out his songs and jokes as well as ever. Yes indeed, it has been no day of rest!

31st July We had more ceremonial on Monday when the AOC and his Senior Air Staff Officer from Group Headquarters arrived to put 605 Squadron through its paces with a view to becoming fully operational once more. Walter has done a first class job training his unit and it naturally came through the tests with flying colours. We would like to believe that Archie McKellar's posting helped, but at all events, we are pleased to see them back on the line and able to take some of the weight off our shoulders for a time.

A few WAAF officers are on strength at Drem, among them Jose MacIndoe, who has been a staunch friend of the Squadron for many years. To mark the occasion of 605's re-emergence to the front line she presented Walter and me with cheques to spend on comforts for the lads. It was a most generous gesture and typical of this attractive, warm hearted girl. However, finding we are already well off for balaclava helmets, mittens, scarves and saucy magazines, I sought Jose's permission to put our cheque into a deposit account as a basis of a benevolent fund for use at a later date. One never knows what would happen to some of the lads if the war should suddenly come to a stop and they found themselves out of a job.

Now that 605 Squadron is working again, I was able to take a day off to visit my parents in Glasgow. However Margaret and I did not wait long, when an over-zealous special constable threatened to run me in for not removing the rotor arm from my car which I had parked outside the flat. He even threatened to let down the tyres! However, as I took pains to inform him, the Germans were welcome to the old Vauxhall, for it is giving much trouble these days and seems to be on its last legs. As it was, we had to drive back to Gullane on three cylinders and ran out of petrol as we drew up outside the gate of the cottage!

Had no sooner got inside when called to the airfield as Dunlop had got caught out in mist while coming in to land and had pranged B in his attempts. One of the aircraft's oleo legs has snapped in two. It is annoying though, for B is our only aircraft fitted with an automatic undercarriage.

Was amused to see five double decker buses parked outside Station Headquarters this morning and surmised correctly that Batchy had been turning his charm on the Head again. Right enough, the wood was swarming with Fettes boys clearing away the remains of the rough undergrowth, dragging felled trees out of the way or helping to build wooden stockades to protect the aircraft from flying splinters. It has just crossed my mind to put in a bid for the derelict fuselage of 'Scylla', as it would make a first class dispersal point in our wooded retreat.

Walter and I reopened the Flying Circus in the evening when we managed to get most of the lads into the air again. Batchy was packing them into the Blenheim six at a time on this occasion!

August

3rd August Batchy has gone to spend a few days with his parents in Yorkshire and has left me in charge of the station. He had not been gone long before the haar rolled in again. In fact, it has been doing this for several days now and one is constantly worrying that the fellows are going to be caught out in the air with insufficient fuel left to divert to other airfields. To make matters worse, we have been warned to expect plenty of enemy activity!

It was on Thursday night when the trouble first hit us. Findlay and Harry Moody had been scrambled after a few plots but had failed to intercept any. However they had been airborne for a considerable time before they were ordered to pancake and both arrived in the circuit none too well-off for fuel. Findlay made three attempts to land through the mist but finally gave up and diverted to Leuchars. However Harry, who had been airborne longer than Findlay, did not have enough juice left for a trip across the Firth, and circled Drem, hoping for a break in the mist, until he was forced to have a got at getting in. Alas he overshot the flarepath and ended up in a hedge at the far end of the airfield, damaging N rather badly. So much for blessing that particular machine last Sunday! Fortunately Harry escaped unscathed.

Woke this morning to find the squadron scattered far and wide. Yellow Section was unable to get back from Macmerry: Green Section was stuck at Acklington, whence it had gone for air firing practice, and Findlay was still fogbound at Leuchars. I believe Batchy would even approve of that form of dispersal! As if that was not enough, a 605 Hurricane also came to grief this morning while landing in the mist. Plonk in the middle of the airfield! And, by sheer coincidence, it was the Hurricane that had appeared at the Blessing Ceremony too! I really must find out what invocation our padre has been calling down on these machines!

More fog is forecast for tonight and I have just spoken to the Sector Commander at Turnhouse to discuss what we should do about the state. Our old Squadron Commander, the Duke of Hamilton, ·has recently taken over as Sector Commander and, being imbued with 602 Squadron intelligence, naturally gave a sensible decision!

'Black everything out and keep the aircraft on the ground,' he said. And how right he is, for we have just heard a Hun passing over, turning round, and going back the way he came. No doubt he couldn't see anything either!

6th August Batchy came back on Saturday and Douglo Hamilton came over from Turnhouse to call on him, as he was wanting to invoke his help in laying on a special night exercise for the guns and searchlights, who apparently have some new gadgets they want to try out. I was detailed to lay on the flying side of the affair and flew Q to Turnhouse on Sunday afternoon to position for the special sortie that night. However, the mist rolled in again, scrubbing the exercise and marooning me over there. However I was well entertained by Betty and Douglo who took me out for dinner instead and gave me a bed and a pair of ducal pyjamas with which to cope with the rest of the night. It was infinitely preferable to flogging the night skies over Lanarkshire!

Whilst transitting back to Drem on Monday morning I overheard the Controller talking to Green Section and vectoring it on to a raid near Arbroath. I called him up to say I would join the Section and reached the area just as Paul was having a go at a Heinkel. Jerry immediately did a stall turn and disappeared into the cloud top when I nipped underneath, hoping to see him come out through the bottom. However, he must have had an attack of shyness, for Jerry never reappeared and the three of us returned to Drem and landed.

We have been trying to think out ways of overcoming some of the problems encountered when flying at night, not least those caused by the exhaust flames. We first tried fitting metal shields above the exhaust stubs, but found they obscured even more than the flames themselves. Then we tried fitting shields made of a perspex material and marking round the burn marks with a chinagraph pencil, using them as templates for metal replacements. In fact, Station Workshops are cutting out a pair right now and I hope to be able to try them tomorrow, weather permitting. Batchy is also playing around with a circle of glim lamps positioned on the normal circuit which, he claims, should lead the chaps on to a proper approach path for landing off. However, these measures will have to remain matters of theory for the moment as the airfield is once again enveloped in fog.

8th August Had to attend a Station Commander's Orderly Room this morning as one of my airmen was on the mat for damaging a Tiger Moth. He had been carrying out a daily inspection on the machine when the silly ass swung the propeller with the switches in the 'on' position and the throttle wide open. The aircraft tipped up on its nose, breaking the prop to pieces. Batchy awarded him 168 hours' detention for his carelessness!

Drem seems to be becoming a centre for budding inventors these days, for we are now working on a ki-gas pump arrangement to squirt glycol on the outside of the windscreens to stop them from freezing up when flying through ice-filled clouds. I got round to testing the device this evening after the mist had cleared and found it worked satisfactorily up to a speed of 180 kts, after which no more juice would come out. We will have to find a way to break down the vacuum which is being created around that speed.

Mickey Mount turned up today fresh from his Spitfire Course, but we have lost another of our old stalwarts, Alastair Grant, who has been posted to a job in Flying Training Command.

605 Squadron is covering the state tonight so I took Mickey and Crackers Douglas to the cottage for a meal. Crackers has recently joined us as Squadron Adjutant. Had to return to camp before the curfew began when we could hear activity going on overhead, and it sounded uncommonly like the unsynchronised growl of Daimler-Benz engines. So Jerry was on the prowl again. Two Hurricanes were already airborne, but the pilot of one called up to say he thought he had a glycol leak and that the smell from the fumes was making him feel drowsy. He has not so far returned, although the other Hurricane landed over an hour ago.

11th August The 605 Squadron aircraft crashed into the sea off North Berwick. The pilot was dead when picked up, having suffered a broken neck. The poor fellow must have been overcome by the fumes.

News from the South is of the Germans keeping pressure on the convoys and the RDF Stations, although the fighter boys are still giving a good account of themselves, but suffering losses nevertheless. I heard a fellow on the wireless the other day broadcasting a live commentary on an action in The Straits, which sounded very exciting. However, I suppose that is what these wireless johnnies are paid to do, although it is an interesting thought that people at home can now switch on their wireless sets and listen to a battle actually taking place.

Had intended to take Q to West Freugh on Friday to fire her guns, but the weather was too bad there and I settled instead for trying out the new ki-gas pump. The freezing level was reported as 11,000 feet and I was therefore pleased to find it operated effectively while climbing through cloud twice that height without any trace of ice forming on the windscreen. Success! I also air-tested the Tiger Moth which has been fitted with a replacement prop!

Another of our chums from Prestwick got married in Edinburgh on Wednesday when Margaret and I were invited. It was the first wedding we had been to since our own last January and, strangely enough, George Reid was Best Man at this affair as well. Poor old George – never the bride! Fortunately we lunched with Finlay and Dorothy Crerar beforehand, because the subsequent Reception turned out to be dry! In fact, I never knew I had such friends!

But it reminded me of a similar disappointment befalling my father some years previously when, on this occasion, the bridegroom had fainted and brandy had been produced to revive him. Dad had lain down beside the groom, hoping! He maintained it had been worth trying! No such luck for us, though, for our bridegroom was as tough as old boots! All in all it wasn't our day, for the fan belt of the car broke on the way home!

We believe we have beaten the night flying bogey at last, for I carried out a combined night test of the flame traps and Batchy's lighting, when both turned out to be effective. I did the flying while Batchy toured the circuit in his car, into which he had fitted an R/T set to enable us to speak to one another, moving the positions of the glim lamps on directions from me until we ended up with an identifiable circuit of lights which eventually led me easily on to the approach path, after which the exhaust baffles allowed a reasonably good view of the flare path ahead. Batchy says he will try to wire up the glims to the Control hut so that they can be switched on and off as required.

Harry Moody and Pat Lyall burst into the crew room at midnight in a considerable state of excitement. They had been in The Royal and heard rumours that 602 Squadron was moving south, so I rang Group to find out more about it.

'Yes,' they said, 'a signal is already on its way to you. You are moving to Tangmere the day after tomorrow!'

12th August You can imagine the flap! All the things to be packed up – manuals, log books, batteries, spares, what-have-yous. Even although we are told it will only be a temporary move, there is still much to be taken. Instructions are for only the first line troops to come with us and for the Squadron Headquarters and Second Line services to remain at Drem. Nevertheless, I intend to take Henry Grazebrook with us, for I am sure there will be business for our Intelligence Officer once we start operating there. Two Harrow transports came in this morning to uplift the troops and equipment and everyone appeared to be fully occupied getting things stowed away, so I took the opportunity to give the ki-gas pump a final whirl to confirm it was still working effectively. It was!

A message was sent to the cottage to the effect that our venue is being changed from Tangmere to Westhampnett, which is a satellite airfield of the former. It makes no difference to us, for at long last we feel we will be seeing something of the real fighting.

13th August Woke to find low clouds and heavy rain, which was hardly an auspicious prospect for our trip to the South. However I found all sixteen Spitfires were serviceable and ready to go. Twelve front line aircraft, plus the four reserves, and I am told the servicing lads worked throughout the night to achieve this hundred per cent turnout. Bless them! The Harrows got away at ten o'clock with everything stowed away in shipshape fashion and the sixteen of us lined up, ready for take-off, two hours later.

I looked round to check that everyone was ready before opening the throttle, and espied Batchy's staff car tucked into the middle of the leading flight, with Padre Sutherland leaning out of the back window blowing his bagpipes for all he was worth! The formation moved forward, the car keeping station until the speed got even too much for our gallant Station Commander to cope with, and the Spitfires were airborne, leaving behind a memorable and touching farewell.

Broke cloud at 15,000 feet only to find that McDowall had had to land again because of engine trouble. However, the remaining fourteen closed in as we headed south, where the cloud cover stretched unbroken for as far as the eye could see. We pressed on hoping for the break that never came, when I decided to find somewhere to land and refuel, for we would have been hard pressed to make it in one. The lads closed in as we let down through the clouds, where we had a bumpy ride until breaking clear at 2000 feet over a murky landscape which I did not recognise. Suddenly an airfield with Spitfires on it loomed up through the gloom. We joined the circuit, were given a green, and landed. By sheer joss I had stumbled upon Church Fenton, so we were well received and given a good lunch by Nick and the boys of 72 Squadron, our erstwhile colleagues at Drem.

We would have liked to have waited at Church Fenton until the weather improved, but 11 Group was urging us to get a move on, saying we were urgently needed in the South as things there were hotting up more than somewhat. So, with aircraft and pilots amply refuelled, we got airborne again and broke into the clear at 10,000 feet as we headed South. We eventually came upon a vast number of balloons sticking through the top of the cloud which gave me a useful indication of our position, as nowhere but London could be that well protected! So I altered course towards the south-west, when the cloud broke up as we neared the coast. At this point we saw a hell of a dog fight going on away to our left but could take no part in it as we were not using the correct R/T frequency and were again running short of fuel. All I could do was to pinpoint Westhampnett and bring the boys in. I must say, I wondered what I had brought them into!

The remains of a Hurricane was lying on its back in the middle of the field, whilst a thick pall of dense black smoke rose from behind the boundary hedge. I was hoping it was not one of ours! However, I was relieved to see the two Harrows had arrived safely and even happier to be marshalled under some trees by one of our own ground crews. A couple of nissen huts seemed to be the only buildings thereabouts.

Johnny Peel, CO of 145 Squadron, was waiting to greet us, for it was his outfit we were here to relieve. He had an arm in a sling. According to Johnny, his outfit had been taking a bit of stick from Jerry and was now reduced to four aircraft and four pilots. That was his Hurricane in the middle of the airfield, he told me. He had brought it down without any aileron control. However, he was glad to say that the smoke rising from behind the hedge was coming from a burning Me 109! Westhampnett was beginning to sound more like Calamity Corner!

The Harrows had by now been reloaded with 145's stuff and took off for Drem again while Johnny and I were talking. Johnny himself left soon after, intending to drive his car to Scotland with only one arm working! I hope he makes it. The four Hurricanes followed, after which we found ourselves the sole occupants of Westhampnett! At least the Jerries seem to have shut up shop for the night, thank goodness.

15th August Jack Boret, Station Commander at Tangmere, came over to welcome us yesterday morning and said we were to call on his station's resources for anything we needed. However, he added, he was sorry they didn't carry any spares for Spitfires as we are the first of that breed they have had in his Sector! Apart from that, just ask for anything you want! That's just great. Thanks very much!

As I have already stated we have Westhampnett to ourselves, but it is nothing more than three large fields knocked into one with the old boundary fences replaced with camouflage paint, similar to that at Dyce. A belt of trees lines the eastern boundary, with two nissen huts nestling underneath. These will do for the A Flight crew rooms. A further two nissens on the north side will house B Flight, but they don't have protection from any trees. As for living quarters, the airmen are billetted in buildings connected to dog kennels on the road to the racecourse, whilst the officers and NCO's have the use of empty farmhouses close to the airfield boundary. I am glad now that I insisted on having our camping equipment put on board the Harrows! Have decided to use one of the A Flight huts for the Squadron Headquarters, as it is nearest the Mess.

We were scrambled seven times throughout yesterday but, while I myself was flying, only intercepted two Blenheims which gave the correct responses when challenged. However Findlay had a brush with a Heinkel off the Isle of Wight in the afternoon and was able to claim a 'damaged'. A massive build-up of clouds probably kept the huns from coming over in large formations, but we were not unduly disappointed, for although tiring, it was a good way to get to know the Sector and how it operates. I took A Flight to Tangmere to cover the night state, but we were not disturbed at all.

We are now operating under 11 Group, whose Headquarters is at Uxbridge, and the local Sector Control is based on Tangmere. We have been told that squadrons in the Group accounted for 157 jerries on Tuesday, for the loss of thirteen of our own aircraft, which makes one realise we are now in the thick of it. Of course, it also makes one realise how close we are to France!

B Flight was already on patrol when we returned from our stint at Tangmere, when they ran into a batch of Do 17's and Ju 88's to the south of Portsmouth but, although they had a go at them, low cloud prevented any positive claims being made. Paul got lost in the melée and I began to think we had had our first casualty. However, he turned up twenty minutes later suffering from nothing more serious than a bad dose of embarrassment at having got himself lost! Findlay said it had been a bad trip, as they had been fired on by the ack-ack batteries from Portsmouth and later set upon by a squadron of Hurricanes while they were returning to base. I suppose that is the penalty of being the first Spitfire squadron in the Sector but I have no doubt they will learn to recognise our shape in time.

Q was overdue for an inspection, so I flew her to Tangmere this evening and stayed for dinner in the Mess with the Station Commander. The place does not seem to have altered much since 602 Squadron did its annual training at Tangmere in 1936. Jack later drove me back to spend my first night in the farmhouse, which seems rather empty, the only pieces of permanent furniture being a fine old dutch dresser and a wooden kitchen table!

16th August It has been quite a day!

It started quietly enough with the squadron stood down for the morning, when I was able to do some work in the office and take a look at the airmen's billets, which are far from satisfactory and smell of dogs. It was as we sat down for lunch the fun and games started.

We were surprised to be given the order to scramble from a state of 'released', but the reason was all too apparent as we rushed helter skelter from the Mess to see thirty Ju 87 dive bombers screaming vertically on to Tangmere. The noise was terrifying as the explosions of the bombs mingled with the din of ack-ack guns which were firing from positions all round us. We could hear the rattle of spent bullets as they fell on the metal covered nissens where we hurriedly donned our flying kit. Chunks of spent lead fell about us as we jinked out to our aircraft. Our crews, wearing steel helmets, had already started the engines and sped us on our way with the minimum of delay. It was a complete panic take-off, with Spitfires darting together from all corners of the field and it was a miracle that none collided in the frantic scramble to get airborne.

I called the boys to form up over base at Angels 2. A Flight was already with me, but there was no sign of B Flight. However, there was no time to stop and look for them! The air was a kaleidoscope of aeroplanes swooping and diving around us, and for a moment I felt like pulling the blankets over my head and pretending I wasn't there! I had no idea it could be as chaotic as this! Selected a gaggle of 110's and dived to attack. Out of the corner of my eye I caught sight of a Spitfire having a go at another 110 and blowing the canopy clean off it. A Hurricane on fire flashed by and I was momentarily taken aback when the pilot of the aircraft in front of me baled out, until I realised he had come from the 110 I had been firing at! Then it was all over. No one else was about.

Some of the lads were already on the ground when I got back and, apart from Mickey, the others turned up within the next five minutes. Mickey had collected a bullet in his coolant tank and had gone down at Odiham.

It is just as well we brought Henry Grazebrook, for Findlay, Dunlop, McDowall, Rose and myself all claimed victories and he was kept at it, writing up the combat reports. I think Findlay's effort was the best of the bunch, for a Stuka pulled out of its dive straight in front of him just as he became airborne, when Findlay pressed his firing button and blew it apart. He said he was so surprised that he merely completed circuit and landed, without even retracting his undercarriage! I don't suppose Findlay had been airborne for more than a couple of minutes!

I drove over to Tangmere in the evening and found the place in an utter shambles, with wisps of smoke still rising from shattered buildings. Little knots of people were wandering about with dazed looks on their faces, obviously deeply affected by the events of the day. I eventually tracked down the Station Commander standing on the lawn in front of the Officers' Mess with a parrot sitting on his shoulder. Jack was covered in grime and the wretched bird was screeching its imitation of a Stuka at the height of the attack! The once immaculate grass was littered with personal belongings which had been blasted from the wing which had received a direct hit. Shirts, towels, socks, a portable gramophone – a little private world

Myself at Owlscote, Upton, 1940 and (*below*) preparing to leave from Harwell, September 1940.

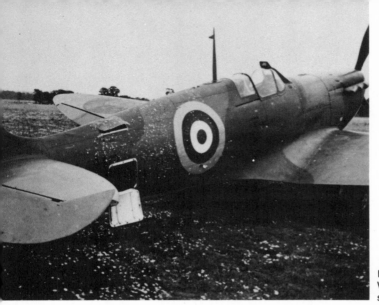

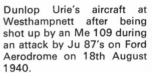

Dunlop Urie's aircraft at Westhampnett after being shot up by an Me 109 during an attack by Ju 87's on Ford Aerodrome on 18th August 1940.

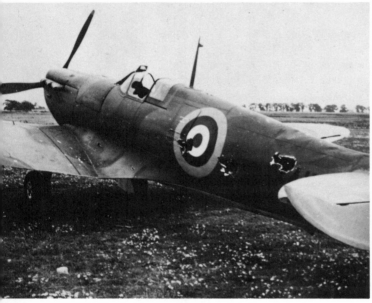

Alastair in trouble.

exposed for all to see lay in profusion around our feet. However, the bar had been spared and was doing a brisk trade!

Tommy Thomson, the Station Adjutant, took me over to the airfield to see the damage. Rubble was everywhere and all three hangars had been wrecked. I managed to crawl under the tangled remains of one of them as I wanted to find out how my aircraft had fared. Alas, a heavy girder had crashed on top of Q, breaking her back and severing one of the mainplanes. I feel very sad about this, for I had grown to love that aeroplane and it was patently obvious that she was only fit for the scrap heap.

Tommy then showed me the remains of the neighbouring hangar and, pointing to its massive door lying flat on the ground, remarked wistfully, 'My Triumph Dolomite is under that little lot. I only bought it last week!'

What could I say?

Four of our aircraft had been in the hangars at Tangmere, and we have lost the lot. The remains of Billy Fiske's Hurricane was still smouldering in the middle of the airfield when I left and Billy himself is in the Station Hospital, gravely injured. Max Aitken and his 601 boys have been having a hard time of it since they came to Tangmere.

Already stories are going around of how the fellows reacted during the aerial onslaught – some patently numbed by the force of it, whilst others seemed to become spurred to greater action by the terrifying enormity of the moment. And the heroes were often those whom one would least expect to stand out among their fellow men. Such a man has been our Medical Officer, Doc Willey, who apparently was doing great deeds throughout the blitz.

The Germans launched heavy attacks against many sites along the South Coast today. Biggin Hill, Kenley, Manston and North Weald have all been thumped.

18th August The changing face of war! Everything seemed quiet and peaceful yesterday after the excitement of the previous day, when I looked out of my bedroom window on to an idyllic scene below. The lawns, which must have taken decades of careful husbandry to get them to their present state of verdant lushness; the fine old trees; the scented shrubs; the birds in song. There was an air of the incongruous about the tranquillity of the scene. I am told that it is even possible to chuck an egg into the air, when it will land on the grass without breaking, although I doubt whether our rations will allow us to try the experiment!

While the boys were taking a breather, I went to Tangmere to have a word with Jack Boret about getting better accommodation for the airmen and also to scrounge some pieces of furniture for our Mess. He was not in his office, but I eventually found him over on the airfield, supervising a crowd of German airmen who were helping to clear up some of the mess they had been instrumental in creating. Fourteen Stukas have been brought down within a few miles of Tangmere and Jack had rounded up their surviving crew members and was now rubbing their noses in it! I doubt whether the Geneva Convention would approve however!

I got a sympathetic hearing from Jack, who promised to have our problems looked into, and returned to Westhampnett, having first picked up a signal announcing that our temporary move had been made permanent! Indeed, two Harrows were already there with our Column 5 stores (those used by the servicing crews), although there was no word of when we could expect the remainder of the Squadron personnel to turn up.

Had only one patrol to do during the night but nothing came of it. However, I was diverted to chase after a stray barrage ballon on the way back this morning and caught up with it at 26,500 feet as it was drifting towards the Portsmouth area. However, I found that a balloon is not the easiest of targets to shoot down, in spite of its size and immobility. To begin with, one has to puncture it on top of the envelope, otherwise the gas won't come out. Secondly, one can neither shoot at it from above, nor use incendiary ammunition for fear of causing casualties on the ground below.

So, I thought, I would climb steeply and attack the thing from underneath, hoping that the bullets would pass clean through from bottom to top, but this time found myself thwarted by the tethering ropes dangling beneath the monster! Out of sheer frustration, I eventually emptied everything into its side, after which the balloon continued its lazy drift towards the Isle of Wight, apparently intact! It was only I who was deflated!

Having been up for most of the night, I handed over to Dunlop for the rest of the day. The squadron had a quiet morning, with no patrols called for, but it was scrambled during the afternoon and vectored to the neighbouring airfield at Ford which was under attack by a gaggle of Stukas with escorting fighters. The boys were jumped by 109's before they could get among the dive bombers, when a hell of a donny developed. In spite of this, they accounted for twelve Stukas, but not without cost to themselves. Dunlop, Mickey, Ian Ferguson, Harry Moody and Sergeant Whall were all clobbered. Mickey and Whall got their damaged aircraft down at Tangmere, Ian hit high tension cables attempting to get down at Merston, Harry baled out and came down in the grounds of a girl's school near Arundel, whilst Dunlop nursed the remains of his Spitfire back to Westhampnett. It was a miracle it still flew, for half its rudder and tail fin had been shot away and one of the elevators had been badly damaged. Dunlop himself has suffered shrapnel wounds in his legs and is in considerable pain. Ian has been taken to hospital in Chichester with a strained back. However the others are back, little the worse for their experience.

19th August The Equipment officer assures me that stocks of Spitfire spares are on order but they have not yet arrived at Tangmere. However, we are urgently requiring certain parts, so I telephoned the CO at Middle Wallop, our nearest neighbours operating Spitfires, and explained our predicament. 'Only too glad to help, old boy,' was the helpful rejoinder, 'Send a lorry over and I will see what we can do!' However, I was more than surprised when our party got back to find enough stuff in the vehicle to build a whole new aircraft! There was sufficient there to keep us going for weeks.

Apparently our lads were nearing Wallop when it came under attack by Stukas, so they pulled up at the roadside and took shelter in a ditch. Whilst they watched the scene, a Jerry floated down on a parachute and they took him prisoner before proceeding to the station as soon as the All Clear sounded. However, everyone appeared too busy putting out fires and so forth to attend to them, so they sought out the Stores Section and proceeded to help themselves.

Having handed over their captive to the Guard Room and saying
'Thank you', they returned immediately to Westhampnett without
further incident. When I rang the Station Commander at Wallop to
thank him for his generosity, his only reply was 'For what?' He did
not know our boys had been there and I only hope he will be able to
write off his missing stores against the raid on his station!

Thorney Island and Portsmouth were visited by Jerry this morning, when we got stuck into a large formation of Ju 88's, three of
which went down before the 109's intervened. They descended on
us like a ton of bricks, after which everything broke up in confusion
and the air became full of flying lead. I felt the thud of a bullet hitting the fuselage but, as my controls were still working OK, was
able to carry on and actually fired short bursts at two 109's, but
with no visible detriment to their airworthiness! I am either a lousy
shot, which is true, or I have started to fire rubber bullets! Poor
Harry copped it again and baled out for the second day running.
However he is back at base already and says he is raring to go!

Had to search around to find where my aircraft had been hit. It
turned out to be on the rudder, but a speedy patching job soon
fixed it.

Led A Flight in the afternoon when we intercepted a solitary Ju
88 as it beat a hasty retreat over the Isle of Wight. Presumably he
was the follow-up recce plane from the previous raid. However, being on its own made it an easy prey and one burst was enough to
pitch him headlong into the sea with an almighty splash. The
Junkers was flying too low for anyone to bale out.

Was delighted to find Crackers and the rest of the boys had arrived when I got back, having travelled down on the overnight train. I
quickly put him in the picture and told him to settle in and then
start looking for better accommodation for the troops. However,
our own accommodation is now looking up, for a number of
neighbours have been calling at the Mess and most have been quick
to offer a loan of furniture and other items for our comfort. 'Just
send along transport', they say.

Bing Cross also looked in today. He is convalescing from his
dreadful experience when *Glorious* was sunk, and when he nearly
lost both his legs from frostbite. He now needs two walking sticks to

help him along. He told me that he and two others were adrift on a raft for a long time before being rescued. He also said he had never heard a noise like it when shells from *Scharnhorst* and *Gneisenau* started to hit the carrier. Apparently *Glorious* went down rapidly, taking most of her complement with her.

Drove Dunlop to hospital in Chichester to have further shrapnel splinters removed from his legs and called in to see Ian Ferguson while there. It would seem that both are going to be out of action for a considerable time. In the meantime, Crackers has been busy and has done a deal with Goodwood Golf Club to accommodate the airmen. He has certainly wasted no time.

21st August Harry and I were at Tangmere yesterday to arrange for parachutes to be pulled and inspected. Not surprisingly, Harry is showing more than the usual interest in this activity now! He allowed me to read a letter he had received from the head girl of the school into whose grounds he had parachuted two days ago, which said that the school had voted to adopt him! It went on to say that the girls were already knitting things for him and wanted to know what was his favourite colour and would he promise to write often to them! Poor Harry! I told him it was the price he had to pay for being so handsome!

Two Bofors guns have turned up to augment the airfield defences, so took time off to help to site them and to look round the security arrangements in general. I must say I was appalled to find it had been sadly neglected and, for instance, that the wooden fence bordering the road is broken in many places and it is possible even to drive a vehicle through them here and there. I have asked Crackers to take it up with Tangmere. Also visited the racecourse for the first time as Freddy Richmond has agreed to let us use space under the grandstand for a storeroom. He says he is not expecting the racing calendar to affect Goodwood for a while yet!

Jack wants me to get as many boys as possible off the station when conditions permit so, after flying on a couple of unproductive sorties this morning, took the hint and entrained at Chichester with Donald Jack and Roger Coverley for a night in London. Southern Railway gave us a marathon ride, stopping at every station as far as

Brighton and only speeding up when the train pointed towards London itself. We thought we were in it for the night! However, we got there in time to have a haircut at Victoria before going along to the RAF Club for a noggin and to cash cheques and then dining at Fischer's Restaurant.

Donald and I spent a comfortable night in The Grosvenor Hotel, Roger having made other arrangements, the nature of which we didn't enquire into! London seems much as usual, although many more people now wear uniform of one sort or another. Most, too, conscientiously carry around their gas masks, although I am told a lot of girls remove the mask itself and use the case instead for a handbag!

23rd August We had a faster journey back yesterday morning and I was in time to go on state at 11.30. The train must have been The Director's Special, because we only stopped twice between Victoria and Chichester. In any case, we were not called on to fly.

Jack brought the Duke of Kent to visit us in the afternoon. HRH is now serving as a Group Captain and is much involved with Welfare. They stayed to tea in the farmhouse after which I took him round the policies where he showed particular interest in the set-up at the Golf Club premises. He did, however, suggest to Jack that we should be allowed transport to take the chaps from the billets to their place of work as they have over a mile to walk. Jack promised to do something about it.

Our friendly neighbours continue to be generous and the farmhouse is rapidly acquiring many comforts. For instance, we have now added three easy chairs, a dining room suite and a coal scuttle, and Crackers tells me he has been offered the use of a Vi-spring mattress and would I like it for my bed! What a damned stupid question. Of course I would! But seriously, everyone has been helpful and kind and I feel the time has come to dismantle the little room to the left of the front door. Until now we have kept only a few broken-down pieces of camping equipment in it and have been steering new callers into it hoping to touch their generosity! It has now done its job!

We encountered a Ju 88 over Portsmouth this morning. It was

darting in and out of broken clouds when Findlay managed to get a burst in on it. However, he had to give up the chase when guns from Portsmouth got him locked on to their sights instead of the Junkers. Furthermore, Ops forgot to tell us there was another fighter squadron operating on this particular raid and we only found out the hard way when Glyn collided with a Hurricane as they both emerged from the same cloud! Glyn was fortunate to get back with a damaged prop and a bent wing tip. The pilot of the Hurricane had to bale out.

A mobile canteen, manned by two charming ladies, Mrs Euan Wallace and Miss Virginia Gilliat, turned up on the field this morning and attracted troops round it like bees round a honey pot. Mrs Wallace and her husband live nearby at Lavington Park, and invited me to dinner this evening, so the least I could do was to purchase a mug of tea and a sandwich!

However, before I left for Lavington, a low flying Ju 88 flashed out of a cloud, roared across the field and then disappeared with equal suddenness. But not a shot was fired at it by our recently installed Bofors! When Pat Lyall and I drove over to the site, we found the gun crews huddled round a wireless set, listening to the evening news bulletin. It is hard to believe, but they not only failed to see the Ju 88 streaking before their very eyes, but they never even heard it! I made up my mind there and then to speak to Jack about our poor ground defences.

Lavington is a beautiful house standing amidst splendid parkland, and its host and hostess could not have been more hospitable. Captain Euan Wallace is commissioner for London, having previously held the post of Minister of Transport in Chamberlain's government. However, I managed to put up a monumental black when coffee was being served, for I helped myself to a whole spoonful of saccharine tablets, thinking they were just some new form of sugar which I had not before come across!

24th August AC2 Wyer has volunteered to be my batman. He is a great little chap who wears large pebble glasses which make him look just like Peter Lorre, the film actor. In fact, he was nicknamed 'Mr Motto' as soon as he joined the unit. He runs a jeweller's business in civvy street but gave it up to come into the Services determined, he said, to make it the RAF in spite of his defective vision. He was told he could only become a batman. So a batman he has become, and a very good one at that. Besides, he makes a jolly good cup of tea!

Jack came over to discuss the Bofors incident, when I pointed out to him our shortcomings in ground defences generally. He said he would attach Flying Officer Macintosh as Ground Defence Officer at Westhampnett, although I must say I have certain reservations about his choice. I had met Mac on a number of occasions and, whilst admitting he is a very nice old fellow, his only visible attribute for the job is a number of campaign medals from the 1914-18 War. However, I had better reserve judgement until he arrives.

The squadron should have been stood down today, but we were nevertheless sent off at short notice to go after some Jerries reported approaching Portsmouth from the South. In fact they were very high up – two hundred of them, flying in at over 27,000 feet, and we could see clearly their vapour trails as we took off. We climbed towards them at full throttle but, when the trails began to swirl and weave strange patterns in the sky, realised the Tangmere squadrons were already in among them. A lot of heavy ack-ack shell were also bursting thousands of feet below the raiders which, in fact, later became more of a menace to ourselves than to the enemy as we climbed towards the activity.

We could also see bombs bursting among the buildings in Portsmouth and Southampton and the increasing number of palls of smoke bore evidence of the tragedy going on below. The bombers were in retreat even before we had reached 25,000 feet and were already well out over the Channel, with the Hurricanes battling it out with the escorting fighters some miles behind. Two 109's sniffed briefly at us as they sped after their cronies, but made no attempt to attack us. We were ordered to pancake immediately afterwards, as Tangmere had been left unguarded.

The news is grim. Goering is throwing large numbers of the Luftwaffe against us, and Fighter and RDF Stations are continuing to be singled out for attack. Aircraft factories too have been added to the calling list and everywhere the strain is beginning to show. I notice people are becoming edgy and short tempered, and one wonders for how long the lads can go on taking it. Yes, things are tough, and today's raid on Portsmouth, for instance, did a lot of damage to the town as well as to installations in the dockyards. Many buildings have been razed to the ground, including a picture house which caught a direct hit during a special matinee for school kids. The railway station has also been badly damaged.

There is little doubt Hitler is preparing to launch an invasion, for crews from the Bomber and Coastal Command squadrons, who are carrying out nightly attacks on Channel ports, speak of large concentrations of barges being assembled in many of them. Local church bells are to be rung if an invasion starts so that everyone will know to stand-to. Everyone is also keeping a surreptitious eye on the wind direction, for many of us believe it would not be unreasonable to expect poisonous gases to be let off as a prelude to the main strike. All in all, it is not a very cheery prospect!

25th August After two frustrating sorties in the morning, when the plots turned tail before coming within range, the squadron was scrambled from a cold start, as it were, during the luncheon break. Once again we had our meal interrupted to dash off to Weymouth at Angels 15. We arrived in time to intercept a sizeable formation of Ju 88's and Do 17's as they crossed the coast, travelling on a northerly course. As usual they had their escorts with them, so I ordered B Flight to take on the fighters whilst A Flight concentrated on the bombers.

Our initial attack split up the bomber formations. Some wheeled away left and right. Some dived steeply, whilst others actually turned tail. In fact, there were Dorniers and Junkers all over the shop, and it soon became a case of every man for himself. I went for one of the Dorniers but was unable to observe the result as the fighters which had eluded Findlay's attention were down among us in no time at all. Earphones filled with shouting – 'Look out behind you!'. 'I've got one!', or simply 'Jeezis Christ!'

I could only leave the boys to it and hope for the best. Besides, I had plenty with which to cope on my own plate. Climbed after a

110 and nailed him from below, when the entire tail unit blew off and the pilot baled out in front of me.

I dived below the melee to take stock and was just climbing to go after a lone Ju 88 I could see some distance off, when I became aware of tracer bullets whizzing past my port wing. Remembering Harry Broadhurst's advice that Germans often used tracers as a sighter, I sideslipped towards it when, as Harry had predicted, it then started to streak past my starboard wing tip. A glance in the mirror showed a 109 glued to my tail and I pulled hard back on the stick to gain height, hoping to force him to pass underneath me. Not him! The 109 stuck to me whilst I climbed, until I ran out of airspeed and did an unexpected stall turn to the left.

My adversary then hesitated, which proved to be his undoing, for by the time he had decided to follow suit, he presented a broadside target only yards away as I assumed the vertical. Even I could hardly miss this time and I watched his canopy shatter into smithereens when the eight Brownings struck it at point black range. The poor fellow did not stand an earthly and the 109 went down in a juddering series of flat spins until it crashed in a ball of flame into a spinney just south of the town of Dorchester. There was no one else in sight when I had time to look around, so I called up and told the boys to find their own way home when they were ready.

There was naturally much excitement at Westhampnett, where some of the lads had landed ahead of me. The refuellers were pumping in petrol as fast as they could; armourers rushing up fresh containers of ammunition; groups of pilots obviously discussing the action, whilst Henry Grazebrook darted among them collecting their stories for inclusion in the combat reports to follow. Our bag was good. Fourteen confirmed, four probables and two damaged. Two of our own blokes are down. Sprague baled out into the sea, but has already been fished out unhurt. Roger Coverley has also had to bale out of his blazing Spitfire, but has been on the phone to say that he too is unhurt. As for myself. Two confirmed in one sortie! Perhaps all my bullets are not made of rubber after all!

26th August Macintosh reported to me this morning, when I explained to him what I wanted done. I told him I wanted the airfield made more secure and suggested he started by taking a look at the perimeter fence. 'Verra guid, surr!' whereupon he toddled off to get on with the job. In the meantime I set about the task of writing reports, for every incident involving one of our aircraft, whether it be shot up, shot down or merely run into by a passing bicycle, requires an explanation in writing from the Squadron Commander. In triplicate! I fear that most of the reports emanating from my office tend to be on the short side!

However I was able to clear them in time to entertain Captain Broome and his wife to luncheon in the Mess. Broome is with Vickers and has been most helpful in many ways, not least by arranging for us to fly aircraft shot up in battle direct to the Supermarine Works near Southampton without having to first land at base. In this case the damaged aircraft has to be dismantled before despatch by road through Chichester and Southampton to reach the repair depot. When our fellows reckon their aircraft will probably need expert attention they fly straight to the works and pick up a reconditioned Spitfire and leave the battered model behind.

True to form, however, Jerry interrupted this lunch too and we were scrambled to go after a raid approaching Portsmouth from the south. The Controller did a fine job of the interception on this occasion and positioned us perfectly, one thousand feet above and up-sun of the target. We spotted them instantly – about fifty or sixty Ju 88's and Do 17's scudding northwards immediately above an unbroken layer of cloud. It was a copybook interception, for the enemy had not spotted us and, so far as we could make out, had come over without a fighter escort. It was almost too good to be true! Furthermore, we got our wires crossed, for we could hear the Huns chattering to each other on our R/T channel.

Having allocated the targets, we dived out of the sun towards our unsuspecting prey. I had chosen to go for the fellow leading the first vic of Dorniers so, lining up my sights on him, pressed the firing button.

Instantly there were agonised shouts on the R/T. *'Schpitfeur! Schpitfeur!'* as Spitfire after Spitfire opened up on the intruders.

My aircraft juddered under the recoil of the guns and I watched the bullets streaking into the distance ahead of me. Dare I admit it, but the fellow leading the *second* vic of Dorniers then keeled over and burst into flames! Not very good shooting, and certainly not what I had intended. However, I suppose it all counts in the long run!

The Germans were obviously taken by surprise and the formation broke up in utter confusion as we dived among them. Ju's and Do's alike, dived for the protection of the clouds in one higgledy piggledy mass. We never saw them again, but I wonder how many collided during that panic scramble for cover.

We were credited with six destroyed and three damaged on this occasion, but not without cost. Hector MacLean stopped a cannon shell on his leg which blew off his foot at the ankle joint. Notwithstanding the extreme pain, Hector kept calm and managed to fly his damaged aircraft back to Tangmere where he landed wheels up in the middle of the field. The brave fellow was still conscious when lifted from his cockpit and carried to the waiting ambulance. Indeed he sent one of the orderlies back into the aircraft to retrieve his shoe – it had been a new pair, he said – when the man in question took one look at what was inside it and passed out on the spot! Cyril Babbage was another casualty. He had to bale out over the sea, but was picked up promptly and brought ashore. He is now in hospital in Bognor suffering from minor injuries to his legs.

McDowall and I toured Selsea Bill in the car this evening, searching for a Heinkel Mac says he shot down during the action. Alas, we could not find it.

28th August Yesterday was peaceful by comparison with the day before and we were wondering whether Jerry was hanging back, licking his wounds, or whether, as is more likely, he was flexing his muscles for bigger things to come. At all events it was quiet when Jack Boret paid a visit, during which we happened to look out of my office window and were astounded to see a family party disporting itself round one of the Spitfires parked on the far side of the field. We drove over to find Mum and Dad unpacking a picnic hamper in the shade of a wing whilst their two children played happily nearby! So much for Macintosh's efforts at making the airfield secure!

But, to give him his due, he had got rolls and rolls of barbed wire and had positioned it along the length of the perimeter. Unfortunately he had laid it so close to the wooden fence that it was a simple matter to climb on to the fence itself and step over Mac's coil of wire!

The old Scot was quite unabashed when we pointed it out to him. After all, he had assured me only last night 'The field is noo verra weel defended, surr!' However, after questioning, he amended his statement to 'Weel, at least the main gate is verra weel defended surr!' Having promised early remedial action, Jack took Macintosh back to Tangmere with him half an hour later!

Doc Willey and I drove to Chichester to see Hector in the Royal West Sussex hospital and found him sitting up in bed as chirpy as a sparrow. His right leg has had to be amputated and he is also sporting a beezer of a black eye, which he said he got when his head hit the windscreen landing. He had undone his safety straps earlier in case he should need to bale out. It is fortunate he didn't, for I doubt whether he would have survived a drop into the sea. In any event, he is in great form and clearly delighted with the calibre of the nurses at the West Sussex and is looking forward to a spot of leave once he can escape their clutches. The fellow has the heart of a lion.

Having assured ourselves about Hector, Willey and I drove on to Bognor to see how our other casualty was coming along and found him ready to be discharged! The medicos had removed some shrapnel from his leg and said he would not take long to heal up again. Unfortunately Cyril's clothes were still damp from sea water, so he borrowed a coat from one of the hospital porters and we brought him back with us to Westhampnett. Even Henry Grazebrook has had a quiet day!

Went back to Chichester for supper in The Dolphin with some of the 43 Squadron boys, but it turned into a rather liquid affair, so much so, in fact, that none of us heard the air raid sirens when they went off sometime during the evening!

30th August I don't know whether the party in The Dolphin had anything to do with it, but I have been off flying for the past two days with griping pains in my tummy which Doc has diagnosed as 'a touch of the trots'! I should say! So I have been able to enjoy the peace of the garden with a deck chair and a book of dubious content. However, the idyllic setting was rudely disturbed yesterday afternoon when Findlay turned up and decided to use an old elm tree as a target for revolver practice. Although Findlay was not so pleased, I personally was much relieved when he was called to lead the squadron on a patrol over Kent. Nothing came of the sortie however, although we have been getting reports of many raids on targets in Kent and on East Sussex.

After again visiting Hector this morning, I met Dunlop off the train on his way back from sick leave in Glasgow. He is still limping badly and thinks he will probably be posted soon from 602 Squadron, but I hope this is not so. Also I have received a letter from the Lord Provost of Glasgow, sending congratulations on behalf of the city where, Dunlop tells me, the unit has been the subject of a lot of publicity in the local Press. The Lord Provost also said he had heard about my efforts to get a Benevolent Fund going for the Squadron and added that he would like to become associated with the project.

This evening two bombs fell close enough to rattle our windows, but no one has been called upon to fly so far. The Hurricanes are doing the state tonight and I gather some aircraft from The Fighter Interceptor Unit at Ford are also coming on state now.

31st August We found a number of unexploded incendiaries lying on the airfield this morning which must have been dropped during last night's activity. I thought it wiser to send for experts from Tangmere to deal with them. I somehow can't see any of my chaps being successful defusers! Am still off flying because of my tum, so got on with the bumff in the office. It is never ending, and now I find I have the Confidential Reports on the officers to complete. At least I won't have to perjure myself overmuch, for they are, one and all, thundering good chaps in any case!

Findlay took the squadron on patrol between Biggin Hill and Gravesend this afternoon and ran into a gaggle of Ju 88's and 109's all mixed up together. This is an unusual configuration for the Germans, for their fighters normally operate some distance above and behind their bombers. At all events, the boys are claiming one Ju 88 and three 109's although Sergeant Elcome collected a bullet in his coolant tank and has had to land at Ford.

Bombs are crumping around us again as I write this, but there have been no reports of damage so far.

September

2nd September The heavy raids over Kent have been on the increase lately and the squadron was scrambled to the London area this morning to lend a hand. However we missed the fun, as there was nothing for us there, and were sent back to base soon after. I am glad to report that I had passed my medical earlier.

At long last I got round to calling on Ralph Hubbard. Ralph, who is factor to the Richmond estates, has been most helpful and has been instrumental in making over all sorts of accommodation for the squadron. I was glad therefore to have an opportunity to thank him personally and to regularise most of our requisitions. Ralph said he had had a message from the Duke of Richmond asking him to give us whatever help we needed, which is a friendly gesture indeed.

This afternoon Harry turned up with one of his old girl friends, a WAAF officer stationed at Tangmere, and we were able to give her tea in the farmhouse. I hope she recognised the significance of the occasion, for we were able to serve it off real china for the first time. In fact, we are becoming thoroughly spoilt as more and more chattels turn up for the Mess, which now boasts a number of carpets and rugs and a few additional pieces of furniture, not to mention a number of smaller items purloined from local pubs, among them being three spitoons. Why three, I don't know, for none is ever used!

Of course, Mr Motto disapproves and he spoke to me about it this morning when he brought my early tea.

'There is yet *another* cuspidor, Sir,' he said.

He always refers to them as cuspidors for he believes he conjures up more disdain by the use of that word. We are also to receive a hangar. A Bessoneau hangar, which is a canvas contraption assembled over a wooden framework. We have decided to have it erected in the field on the other side of the road, although we will have to dismantle some of Mac's barbed wire entanglement to get the aircraft across the road. At least the maintenance boys will be able to work on the aircraft with some shelter over their heads when it goes up.

Henry's WAAF must have enjoyed her tea, for she invited Henry and me to sup with her in the WAAF Officers Mess at Tangmere this evening. The girls are snugly housed in the little cottage directly opposite the main gate, the same cottage John and Rachael Willoughby occupied when he was at Tangmere with 605 Squadron earlier. I gather King Leopold used to visit them there.

Nuts Niven posted in today, but I fear we will have to give him a quick conversion on to Spits as he has only been trained on Hurricanes.

3rd September Spent an agonising half hour this morning watching Nuts juggling with a Spitfire but, to his everlasting credit, he and the aeroplane both finished up in one piece. However, two further pilots, Pilot Officers Payne and Hanbury, have come to us straight from a Lysander squadron with no experience whatsoever on fighter aircraft. Apparently demand has now outstripped supply and there are no trained pilots available in the Training Units, which means that we will just have to train them ourselves. However it remains to be seen whether we can spare the hours, as we are already short of aircraft for our own operational needs. It seems a funny way to run a war.

Had a rather unproductive afternoon patrolling the Dover – Eastchurch area, for all we encountered were three squadrons of our own Hurricanes. Most disappointing. Similarly on the dusk patrol, when all we met were a couple of Blenheim squadrons on their way across The Channel to attack German-held ports on the French coast. These boys are having a hard time and their casualty rate has been increasing nightly, as have the rumours of invasion.

We have made such strides with the Mess that we were able to invite Frank Carey and some of his 43 Squadron colleagues to dinner this evening, when they expressed themselves satisfied with the standard of cuisine in the farmhouse. Maybe they were just being polite!

4th September Jack seems to think the invasion will happen any day now and came over this morning wearing a worried expression. He wanted me to break out our holding of small arms and to issue them to the appropriate troops. He also apologised for not having followed up the Duke of Kent's request to provide transport for the airmen and suggested I sent a driver to Tangmere straightaway to pick up something from the S.Ad.O. The outcome of both instructions turned out better than I anticipated.

I know our establishment of small arms is fifty but, when the muster was called, no less than eighty five men paraded with their rifles. When questioned whence came the additional thirty five, the looks of innocence would have done credit to a religious drawing! However it is good to know that the boys in 602 are more than capable of looking after their own, but I still cannot help wondering which units are going short.

Our MT Corporal was equally lucky for, when he duly reported to Daddy Drudge to pick up another piece of transport, he was told there was none to spare. Drudge is a resourceful man, however, and immediately repaired to the main road where he stopped the first Southdown double decker which came along. Having decanted both passengers and crew at the roadside to await the next bus, and having handed the bemused driver with an official receipt for his vehicle, our corporal turned up 'Special' on the signboard and returned to Westhampnett with the latest requisition. Even Jack was taken aback. However, having been around while Nuts had been wrestling with the Spitfire, Jack suggested he might be more gainfully employed in 601 Squadron, as Max Aitken was also short of trained pilots for his Hurricanes.

The Tangmere Wing is becoming more involved in the fighting over Kent and Sussex these days and we found ourselves giving high cover to 601 and 43 Squadrons over Beachy Head this afternoon. There was heavy cloud in the area which can make it harder to pick out the escorting fighters. It can also have the disquieting effect of freezing up the guns as one flies through them. As it is most embarrassing to be caught out with one's guns frozen solid when about to go into action, it has become normal practice, when this might happen, to give them a preparatory squirt before taking on the enemy.

On this occasion we broke into sunshine at 15,000 feet when the Hurricanes made a bee-line for the Dorniers whilst we made for the escorting 110's which we could see circling some miles behind the bombers. I gave my guns the usual test firing and noticed one of the 110's peeling off and diving towards the sea with a lot of smoke pouring from it. The squadron split up in the dog fight which followed but my only contribution to the action was to fire the last of my ammunition at a 110 just before it disappeared into a cloud. I reckoned he was too far off for my shooting to be effective, and returned to base, where we all landed safely.

The boys had shot down three 110's between them but I reckoned it had been one of my rubber bullet days and did not claim any success. 'But what about the one that went down at the beginning?' they said. 'It was you who fired your guns. None of us did.' I wasn't going to argue, but it seemed a jammy way to notch up a victory. The Hurricanes had a field day. They bagged six.

A Flight encountered a formation of 113's this evening but they turned tail as soon as the Spitfires approached. This is the first time we have met this particular type.

Although the enemy has been active tonight we have not been called on and I was able to get over to Lavington for another sumptious dinner. I was glad to see that the bowl of saccharine tablets had been replenished!

5th September Got through a lot of office chores this morning before calling on the Senior Controller to discuss problems connected with the Ops Room telephone. Unfortunately the GPO has not yet been able to give us a proper switchboard and we are still making do with an old field telephone which requires a little handle to be wound to make the bell ring. The boys are becoming fed up with the present arrangement which depends on a certain number of rings, depending on which point is being called. As it was, one ring called A Flight, two rings B Flight, three to alert both flights together, whilst four rings would put you through to the Officers' Mess. This, of course, was playing havoc with the nerves, as each flight in turn, then both flights together, leapt to their feet only to find, on the fourth ring, that it was the Controller calling the cook to enquire what was on the menu for lunch. I am pleased to say that the Mess is now favoured with one tintinabulation only.

Virginia was in charge of the tea waggon today and brought along a most attractive helpmate in Jane Kenyon-Slaney. Mickey and I did our stuff and invited them to lunch in the farmhouse, hoping thereby to be able to jump the queue from now on. Not unnaturally, everyone is most impressed with the service provided by this YMCA team of helpers, who turn up in all conditions. They have never let us down yet, whether we are in the midst of a rain storm, or even under attack from enemy bombers. They are simply great.

Only did one sortie today when I took the squadron to patrol over Biggin Hill at Angels 20. However there was no trade up there and I returned to find Mr and Mrs MacLean had turned up in Chichester to visit Hector. I have arranged to dine with them in their hotel. Let's hope the bombing will let up for them although, from the sound of things, Portsmouth seems to be taking a bit of a hammering as I write this.

6th September A Flight dispersal is situated sufficiently close to the Mess for the chaps to be able to nip over to it when needed, but not so that of B Flight, which is sited some way off on the north side of the field. So, for obvious reasons, we have had a small wooden hut put up containing an Elsan thunderbox. It is much in demand, especially in the early mornings, but one of our members has, alas, not yet weaned himself from his peacetime habits and still makes a lengthy session of it, with morning newspapers and all. Findlay has been griping about this for some time and decided it was time to take action against the offender. So waiting until the culprit was comfortably installed inside the eyrie, Findlay taxied his Spitfire in front of the small edifice, turned the aircraft tail on to it, and opened wide the throttle. I really must have something done about having the hut more firmly secured to the ground!

Led three sorties today, but the first came to nothing after patrolling for some time over Horsham at 20,000 feet. However, the second turned out to be more interesting when we were sent over Mayfield to intercept an outgoing raid then reported to be turning south over the Thames estuary. The Jerries had travelled some distance before we got there, for we caught sight of them in the sunlight many miles to the south of us. We gave chase and were gaining on them in fine style when I suddenly woke up to the fact that we were fast approaching Calais and that dozens of German fighters had come up to escort their chums home. We did a quick about turn and beat it for home, with a horde of angry Messerschmitts hard on our heels.

They caught up with us too, when a general ding-dong ensued, in the course of which Glyn's instrument panel was shot away. Fortunately for Glyn, Sergeant Proctor intervened and downed the 109 as it turned to finish him off. Pat Lyall had a brush with another, but the result was inconclusive. The Spitfires and Messerschmitts then parted company and we went our separate ways and were able to escort Glyn's crippled Spitfire back to base. I fear Glyn has collected a fair amount of shrapnel in his legs as a result of this action and now reckons France is a dashed inhospitable place!

We were sent off again at dusk to patrol Biggin Hill–Kenley where the air seemed to be full of bursting anti-aircraft shells. I think they must have been firing at us, for we saw no signs of enemy aircraft. Findlay has been awarded a DFC today, so I am about to go to the Mess to take a mug of ale off him.

7th September The Germans are evidently not early risers, for we have had another morning free from flying and I was able to nip into Chichester to visit Hector and Glyn in hospital. Glad to say they both seem to be doing well. I also saw our double decker parked outside Woolworth's with 'Chichester' run up on its destination board, so presume Flight Sergeant Connors has been organising a shopping expedition for his lads.

After a leisurely lunch, we were called to readiness at two o'clock when Jack came into the dispersal with the Chief of the Air Staff, Sir Cyril Newall. They had no sooner arrived when the squadron was ordered to patrol Hawkinge at Angels 15. It had been a very warm day and a heavy heat haze hung above the ground to a height of 17,000 feet or more. We soon caught up with the Tangmere Hurricanes and got to the patrol area in double quick time. We have an advantage over the boys operating from further east in this respect, as we are able to climb straight out of Tangmere, whereas the others have to climb to height in a spiral.

We nearly jumped out of our cockpits when we emerged through the top of the haze, for all we could see was row upon row of German raiders, all heading for London. I have never seen so many aircraft in the air all at the same time; there must have been hundreds of them; Heinkels, Dorniers, Junkers, Messerschmitts; you name them, and they were there for as far as the eye could see.

The escorting fighters saw us at once and came down like a ton of bricks, when the squadron split up and the sky became a seething cauldron of aeroplanes, swooping and swerving in and out of the vapour trails and tracer smoke. A Hurricane on fire spun out of control ahead of me while, above and to my right, a 110 flashed across my vision and disappeared into the fog of battle before I could draw a bead on it.

Everyone was shouting at once and the earphones became filled with a meaningless cacaphony of jumbled noises. Everything became a maelstrom of whirling impressions – A Dornier spinning wildly with part of its port mainplane missing: A stoutly built German floating past on the end of a parachute, his arms held above his head in an attitude of surrender: Black streaks of tracer ahead, when I instinctively put my arm up to shield my face: Taking a breather when the haze absorbed me for a moment: Vainly searching for another Villa aircraft.

On edging up through the haze again, was horrified to see the waves of bombers still driving inexorably towards London with no sign of the end of the incoming formations. There was only time to have a quick burst at a passing Heinkel before the 109's were on top of me again as I dived for the protection of the haze.

Tried flying towards the east, hoping to get in on the flank but even there, when I gingerly poked my nose through the top, the hordes were still overhead. And so were the escorting fighters! We were over the Thames Estuary as I squirted at two more passing bombers, but I did not wait to observe the results of the attacks. By now, fires were rising from Tilbury and other docks further up river.

A glance at the gauge told me fuel was running low, so headed for home to replenish before returning to rejoin the battle. As I did so, three 109's passed in front of me from the starboard quarter and I got in a good burst on the nearest one, which immediately rolled its back and dived from sight. When the others turned to attack me I pressed the firing button, but was taken aback to find I had run out of ammunition. This was rather awkward, as these two Jerries apparently had taken a dislike to me and were on my tail before I could say Jack Robinson.

By now I had the Spitfire pointing downhill, with my foot on the throttle and waving for all I was worth, but a glance in the mirror told me the worst. Two yellow-nosed Messerschmitts were on my tail and seemed to be glued to the slipstream for, it didn't seem to matter how much I jinked and dodged, they clung to me like leeches. The altimeter was unwinding like a clock gone mad and it was not until I pulled out of the dive at about a thousand feet, and looked in the mirror, that I noticed the two Charlies had left me. Mind you, it was hardly surprising, as I was heading straight into the Slough balloons!

For once in my life the old brainbox reacted correctly. I saw at once that we were approaching the A4 road out of London and reckoned that not even the balloonatics would be daft enough to fly their balloons from the middle of the road so, having throttled back and put down the landing flaps, I was able to follow the curves of the road and emerge unscathed at the far end of the barrage.

Six gallons of fuel remained in the tank when I landed.

Sir Cyril had waited at dispersal for our return and I was able to give him a first hand impression of the raid. He looked grave and, after a few words with Jack, got into his staff car and drove off. Jack said C. A. S. was going straight back to his office as he was very perturbed to hear that London itself was under attack. It still is being attacked, as far as I know, and it is now after eleven o'clock.

It was very difficult to assess claims in a shemozzle like that as everyone shot at something, but no one can claim more than one or two 'Damaged'. Doubtless we have done better, but are not worrying about that at the moment. It is more important that neither Harry Moody nor Roger Coverley has returned from the sortie, nor is there any news of them. Also, Hanbury and Aries have both been shot down and have crash landed in fields near Maidstone. And what of London itself? I for one would not like to have been there when that load was dropped.

Three new pilots have been posted in today, Pilot Officers Eady, Barthropp and Fisher, and Paul has become a flight lieutenant.

It has been a black day, and the threat of invasion hangs heavily over us.

9th September Yesterday was Sunday and the Germans left us alone all day, although I hardly think it was out of any sense of religious fervour on their part: It is more likely that they, like us, were licking their wounds after Saturday's donny. That raid has left us with much to ponder over, for the forces they sent against London were enormous by any standards. Besides, we still have no word about Harry and Roger, and are beginning to fear the worst. However, I suppose there is always hope so long as there is no news, and I just hope the squadron's luck is not now going to run out. We have been very fortunate so far for, apart from our wounded, we are still all in the land of the living and raring to go.

We were still untroubled by the enemy this morning, although we carried out two routine patrols, both of which turned out to be against X-raids. However, the fun started about tea time when ordered over Mayfield at Angels 15 and arrived in time to see a sizeable force of Dorniers being split asunder by a squadron of

Hurricanes. It was a well executed attack and thrilling to watch. One minute there was this threatening armada thundering towards London; the next it was as if a fox had pounced into a chicken run when everything became a turmoil of fluttering wings and panic reigned supreme. The Germans scattered in all directions and, of course, we got our pickings.

Soon had my sights on a Do 17 when its crew did not wait to argue as I fired the guns. They baled out at once and I just caught a glimpse of three parachutes beginning to open. I was feeling very pleased with myself. Too pleased, in fact, for I did not see the 109 on my tail. Thank goodness Pat Lyall did, though, and another 109 bit the dust. I reckon I owe Pat a double for that one! Also saw one of our Spits pull away with smoke streaming from it, but it was too far away to identify who was flying it. Besides I was then after another retreating Dornier and was able to get a long range shot at it before returning to base.

Have just been to see what is left of Paul's aircraft, for it was him I had seen pulling away from the fray. He had been set on by three 109's which had chased him to ground level, when the poor chap came off second best in the ensuing encounter. By the time they had finished with him, Paul was left with no rudder control, both ailerons severely damaged and flying much too low to bale out. He therefore did the only thing possible and aimed the aircraft straight ahead until he hit the ground.

A clear swathe has been cut through the copse. One comes first upon the port mainplane snarled up in the treetops then, a little further on, the starboard plane which had been torn off at treetop height but which has now fallen to the ground. A large chunk of fuselage comes next, then the engine with the prop still attached, but the cockpit section does not become visible until one has proceeded at least fifty yards beyond the copse itself. It was here they found Paul, semi-conscious and swearing like a trooper. He must bear a charmed life, for he has got away with multiple cuts on the head, a broken wrist and four broken fingers, which will doubtless keep him out of action for some time.

Sergeant Whall is down near Arundel, but he only has a cricked neck.

10th September Woke up to a cold, wet, day which is just what the doctor ordered, for there is less likelihood of the enemy operating in strength when the weather is bad. Besides, it gave the lads a breather, which they badly needed, as there is quite a bit of tension in the air nowadays with everyone expecting the invasion to be upon us at any time. In fact the local church bells were rung the other night, but it turned out to be a false alarm. Indeed, I can't help thinking that we would be more likely to get wind of it before the vicar unless, of course, he is in receipt of information from his own Higher Authority! At all events, we are taking no chances and are now sleeping at the dispersals. In view of the weather, patrols have been reduced to Section strength and, after taking Red Section on an abortive sortie to 18,000 feet, I handed over to Mickey at midday.

Made an effort to visit the wounded at St. Richard's this afternoon, but arrived there to find the hospital in a turmoil as it is under orders to evacuate to a safer area, in common with most other hospitals on the south coast. Hoping to catch them before they left, I raced to the railway station, but got there just in time to watch the hospital train pulling out.

Found a signal waiting for me announcing Mickey's promotion to flight lieutenant, so I have appointed him to run A Flight vice Dunlop, who is about to be posted from the unit. There was also another giving news that Sergeant Whall has won a DFM, which, I must admit, surprised me, for I had not appreciated how well he has done. Gongs seem to be issued almost automatically these days when Group puts in for them whenever a fellow gets six victories. A bar comes along after twelve, and so on. I am not sure it is the fairest system, for many brave lads do great things which go unnoticed and unsung.

Red and Green Sections airborne this afternoon and made contact with a number of Do 17's, but lost them in the heavy clouds. Mickey was again airborne at dusk with Hanbury and Elcome and, although I rang the Controller to warn him that none was night operational, they were kept in the air until it became fully dark, when all three came to grief trying to get down. Two ran off the end of the runway at Tangmere, while Elcome fetched up in a tree at

Felpham. He is now awaiting collection from hospital whilst his aircraft has been declared a write-off.

12th September The volume of enemy trade seems to be falling off lately but, when it comes, it seems to be in penny packets of twenty or so at a time. Strangely too, some of the batches are comprised of fighters on their own.

I had a quiet morning yesterday when on the state, but Mickey ran into trouble when A Flight mixed it with fighters during a small raid on Portsmouth in the afternoon. Although they succeeded in downing four 109's Rose got shot up and Sprague was shot down and is now posted missing. The poor lad was only married two weeks ago.

We are running short of aeroplanes and pilots in the Sector. For instance, I can only raise five aircraft and crews whilst the two Hurricane squadrons have only seven aircraft between them. If anything, I believe the shortage of pilots is the more serious and I have had to recall Findlay from leave. I had expected him back yesterday but he got caught up in the raids on London where, he tells me, the bombing is playing havoc with the transport system. Apparently both Waterloo and Victoria railway stations are out of action, most bus services have stopped running, and the only means of transport is by Underground which, he was at pains to point out, does not yet run to Chichester! He was actually waiting for a train at Victoria when a bad raid started, so he stayed on to lend a hand with the ARP boys. He says the capital is beginning to look tawdry but that its inhabitants are remarkably cheerful, if a trifle slaphappy. At all events, I am glad to see him back. Southampton also had a hammering last night and they say the Town Hall is the only public building left standing.

Something must have gone wrong with Group's adding machine for it appears I have been awarded a DFC. The news must have travelled fast, too, for Barbie Wallace rang up yesterday afternoon to offer her congratulations and to invite me to dine with her and Euan at Lavington last night.

Took my tunics into Chichester this morning to have the ribbons sewn on and called on Glyn to find out how he was progressing. I found him in much pain and the medicos are still digging out pieces of shrapnel from his legs.

Was scrambled to patrol base at Angels 20 this afternoon, but nobody turned up and now I have brought Blue Section to Tangmere for the night state and all is quiet so far.

Doc Willey has won a Military Cross for his efforts during the blitz on Tangmere. We are all delighted, but think it is a strange decoration for a Royal Air Force officer to get.

13th September It was raining heavily when we flew back from Tangmere after doing the night state, and it continued to rain throughout the morning, which gave us a much needed respite. In fact, no patrols were possible until late afternoon, when the weather cleared up. By the time darkness fell, a bright full moon had risen and we reckoned that conditions appeared to ideal for launching invasions!

'So what?' we thought. 'Let's risk it!' and Findlay, Donald and I nipped off to Bognor to visit our favourite pub there, The Victoria. Either the proprietor really knows his business or is in possession of an effective crystal ball, for there is never any shortage of booze in that establishment and it is still possible even to get a number of exotic Continental drinks if one wants them. Besides, we like Hilda. However, we encountered some difficulty getting back into camp as we were continually challenged by our troops doing guard duty who pretended they did not know who we were, and who threatened to march us straight off to the guard room! I suspect an element of sour grapes in this, but I can't say I blame them. Their conditions are very uncomfortable, and I am sure they, too, would enjoy a night out.

14th September Big moment for me when I was ordered to lead the whole Tangmere Wing today – all twelve of us! Five Spits from Westhampnett and seven Hurricanes from Tangmere, that was all we could muster. In fact, I led them on two sorties, but nothing came of either. We merely stooged around Biggin Hill for an hour on the first without coming across anything hostile, and ran into five other Hurricane squadrons over Dover on the second. It is encouraging to know that we have that number left! On one occasion we spotted a number of 109's flying far above us, probably at 32,-000 feet or more, but decided to leave them alone, for Hurricanes and Spitfires are beginning to run out of oomph at these heights.

Was meant to be dining in style tonight but things went sadly amiss. The Duke and Duchess of Norfolk had invited Gini and me to dine at Arundel and I had to pick her up at Lavington to drive her over. The journey entailed a cross country run over a number of narrow country roads. The night was overcast and a number of sporadic air raids were happening along the coast. We were running late and speeding it up a bit and, as we sped round a bend, an aircraft whizzed low over our heads and dropped a bomb nearby which nearly blew the car off the road.

I immediately doused the headlights and had to swerve violently soon after to avoid hitting an unlit cyclist, when the car left the road, rolled down the embankment, and came to rest on its roof.

Having disentangled Gini's legs from around my neck and making sure she was not hurt, we repaired to a nearby pub which appeared to be full of jolly farmers. Naturally, they immediately fell for Virginia and offered help while I telephone His Grace to tell him about our mishap. Bernard thought it a hell of a joke and observed dryly that, if I was able to get the girl on her back before dinner, what earthly hope was there for her once it was over! However, I gather we will be invited again.

Someone turned up with a tractor and we soon had the car back on the road, although its wheels looked decidedly knock-kneed and the radiator not very good for holding water. The landlord loaned us a pail with which to fill up every few miles and I was able eventually to return Virginia to Lavington and bring the Humber back to Westhampnett. Our MT lads say they can repair the damage locally.

Apparently there have been nuisance raids up and down the coast this evening at Littlehampton, Worthing and Bognor. I hope the Victoria is still standing.

15th September Patrolled between Mayfield and Beachy Head this morning in company with 607, but there was nobody about. The

Under-Secretary of State for Air and Jack were waiting for us when we got back and accepted our invitation to stay for lunch. Captain Harold Balfour is a charmer and himself a fighter pilot from the Great War, thus assuring himself of a genuine welcome not normally accorded to our political masters. He is also a friend of Euan and is staying with the Wallaces at Lavington for a few days. Fortunately I was just in time to stop him from making a comment about last night's little episode, for I don't want the Station Commander to find out about the mishap in case he should decide to take the car away. Must say I was relieved to get his conspiratorial wink from across the table.

Sent to patrol over Biggin Hill this afternoon where we ran into a formation of unescorted Dorniers. This was a piece of cake, and we had five down before the rest were able to take refuge in the clouds. We also met several other squadrons of Spits and Hurricanes, which is indeed encouraging, for until recently we have only been coming across aircraft with swastikas painted on them. None of our chaps suffered any damaged in the engagement.

Roger Coverley's body has been found in an orchard near Tunbridge Wells, but there is no sign of his aircraft. Roger had been severly burned and it would seem that he has baled out of his burning aircraft.

17th September The climate is unpredictable. The day began with low clouds and a fair amount of rain but, as it wore on, the rain stopped while the wind got up, and continued strengthening, until we are now in the throes of a full gale! If it does nothing else, it should deter anyone from setting sail from France in a flat-bottomed barge! Nevertheless we were sent off after a bandit, in the Winchester area, I believe, but we were unable to identify our position accurately as we were flying above unbroken cloud throughout. At any rate, something must have gone wrong with the plotting system, for we made no interception and ended up in a classic ogo-pogo.

Was delighted to see Padre Sutherland's cheery face greeting us on return and he tells me he will be staying for a week. After tactful enquiries, was relieved to learn he has left his bagpipes at Drem!

Findlay and I have arranged to do day about from now on, as there is little point in both of us sweating our guts out at the same time. Besides, the pattern of operating is changing and most of the sorties are being done at section strength. In fact, we are beginning to wonder whether we may not have put a dent in Goering's armour after all. Let us hope so anyway.

Findlay got away with Red Section this afternoon and ran into a singleton Ju 88, but it managed to elude them in the clouds. He reported the weather over Woolwich was very bad and that they were lucky to get back to base.

Mickey and I were at Lavington this evening, where we were wonderfully entertained as usual. Gini, who is an accomplished pianist, played for a while but gave up when Mickey found a ukelele and tried to provide the accompaniment. We have suggested he sticks to the gramophone in future!

18th September There was a bright moon up this morning and Findlay got the dawn patrol off half an hour earlier than usual and handed over to me on landing. It is my day on.

Sent to Gravesend with 607 this morning to intercept a raid approaching from the south-east. On climbing through 21,000 feet, we were jumped from behind by some 109's and 190's which we never saw coming. Bloody careless, especially as one of Jimmy Vick's boys went down in the attack before we could even turn to face the onslaught. In fact, they never stayed to fight it out and Jerry left the scene as quickly as he had arrived. In a flash. Bam-bam, and off into the hazy sun. We have no idea what they were up to, for there was no sign of any bombers for them to escort unless, of course, they were well adrift from their charges. However, quite fortuitously, we ran into a single Do 17 on our way home, and gave it the works.

The Dornier rolled on its back and spiralled down with both engines streaming smoke and flames. Three blokes got out, but I did not see any parachutes opening.

We left Henry Grazebrook to sort out what it had all been about.

607 and 602 again joined forces in the afternoon when sent to patrol over London. We thought this an odd patrol position, for

there is normally a lot of ack-ack there. However, it must have been a false alarm, for nothing showed up, not even the guns, and we were ordered to pancake soon after getting there. I spoke to Jimmy over the R/T before 607 peeled off for Tangmere and arranged to meet him later in The Dolphin. I thought it was time we swopped ideas about what the Hun was up to, for he has been behaving in an unorthodox fashion recently.

Jimmy is as puzzled as I am about our foe's behaviour and our evening together brought nothing new to light. We took in the local cinema before coming home and saw Sir Cedric Hardwicke in *The Return of the Invisible Man*. I enjoyed the film, for I have not been to the pictures for months.

19th September Was in the throes of catching up with the paper work when the padre looked into the office this morning. Am always glad of an excuse to dodge the bumff, so offered to show him round the billets and to take him to see Ian Ferguson, who has now been transferred to Goodwood House. Freddie's ancestral home has now been turned into a convalescent hospital, which is very pleasant for the inmates. It is also handy for us, as the main gate is only across the road from the farmhouse. Ian was glad to see us but does not seem to be making much progress. He is still having a lot of trouble with his back.

Gini turned up in the waggon with yet another attractive helper. Very petite. This time it was Pauline Wynn and, as I was on stand down today, took them to supper at The Old Ship Inn at Bosham. Trevor and Nanki Moorehouse run this delightful little restaurant as a club. It sits on the edge of the creek and, when the tide is in, it is possible to sit on the balcony and fish for eels which Nanki is sometimes prepared to cook on the spot, if she happens to be in the right frame of mind. The place was quiet tonight, the only other diner being David Niven, whom Gini knew and who joined us for coffee later. I was interested to meet this famous film star, who was every bit as charming off the screen as on it.

The threat of invasion must be receding as we have reverted to Alert Two today. At least it means we can sleep in our own beds again.

(*Left*): Hilda Godsmark of Victoria Hotel, Bognor.
(*Below*): Pedro Hanbury, West-hampnett, 1940.

Officers' Mess, Westhampnett, August 1940.

A Flight Dispersal, Westhampnett, August 1940.

Johnstone landing, Westhampnett, November 1940.

At Dispersal, Westhampnett, November 1940.

At the Palace with Sir Patrick and Lady Dollan.

September 1940.

20th September The wind has risen again, making it difficult for pilots under training, as the Spitfire's undercarriage is somewhat narrow and it makes the machine liable to coup on to a wing when landing cross wind. Nevertheless the tyros seem to be taking it in their stride.

Was again given the task of wing leader and took the three squadrons into the Biggin Hill area where we saw lots of 109's high above us, but nothing at our level. Stories are going around that the Germans have recently come up with an improved version of the 109, the 109E, with better engine performance, so I reckoned that was what we were watching upstairs. We left them to cavort among themselves, as they were doing no one any harm and we would only have been at a disadvantage if we had tried to go after them. However, the enemy is using new tactics, but they are difficult to understand.

The Wing was ordered to split into flights and to carry out a wide sweep of the Sector on our way home, as Control had a plot on their table for which they were unable to account. We challenged a Harrow over Surrey and forced it to land at Farnborough, but have no idea if this was the aircraft Control was looking for.

Returned to find two distressed ladies at dispersal, their tea waggon having broken down, when our immediate reaction was one of thankfulness that it had not happened elsewhere! Gini and Lavinia Norfolk were forced to have lunch with us and complimented us on the standard of our messing. If the cook finds out he will be demanding that we approach the AA for a two star rating at least!

Jane and Pauline also came for drinks this evening, after which Mickey and I took them to The Ship for supper, where we found Jack Boret, Eddie Ward and David Lloyd already there, entertaining the entire Waafery from Tangmere. Jack was in one of his expansive moods and has granted me week-end leave.

22nd September It is great to get away from the hurly burly of operations for a couple of days. Jimmy Vick has loaned me his Magister in exchange for the Humber (Now repaired!) and I have flown to Harwell to spend the week-end with Ian and Muriel Forsyth. Ian is an old school chum now doing his war service as a navigator in the RAF, and has been fortunate to have his wife with him whilst stationed at this training base.

We dined at a riverside pub at Streatley and spent the rest of the evening having a cosy chat round the fire in their rented cottage at Upton, when Ian brought me up to date with his family news. I was particularly interested to hear about younger brother Derek's exploits with a Commando unit, when his outfit went across the Channel to carry out a raid on a casino where a number of high ranking Wehrmacht officers were known to frequent.

As the Commandos entered the hall with guns blazing, Derek was more than somewhat taken aback to recognise a girl he knew among the assembled company, and took her away from the firing line. What happened immediately after remains obscure, suffice to say he failed to turn up in time to withdraw with his colleagues and was posted missing until he turned up two days later, having been picked up from a dinghy in mid Channel! This sort of adventure makes our life seem humdrum by comparison.

The luxury of a real bed with clean linen sheets must have been too much for me, for I did not surface until midday! It is so pleasant to get away from the sound of aircraft – and from the continual ringing of the telephone.

24th September Back at Westhampnett feeling much refreshed. I think Jimmy was reluctant to hand back the Humber when I delivered his Magister this morning, but we were mutually relieved to find both still in good working order. Was eager to find out what had been going on in my absence.

Pat Lyall and Pedro Hanbury have been busy and had downed a Ju 88 near Bosham on Sunday. Apparently the boffins are very interested in the special equipment it was carrying and we have had a strawberry from the AOC for delivering into their hands. Other news:– The padre has returned to Drem. McDowall has got a DFM, and we have come back to Alert One. Thank goodness I managed to have those two nights between clean sheets!

The squadron flew fifty five hours today, mostly on Section patrols, when Pat Lyall again made the news by having a brief tangle with a new type of Ju 88, which I think the Germans call a Jaguar. They claim it can easily outpace a Spitfire, which I doubt, but be that as it may, Pat was able to fire at it before it disappeared into a cloud.

Jack insisted on taking a crowd of us to The Ship this evening to celebrate his promotion to Group Captain. As the law now requires all places of entertainment to close down by ten o'clock, it inevitably became a session of concentrated severity!

25th September The weather is turning distinctly colder and I am beginning to wish I had brought some winter woollies. However, I was only flying on a low level patrol this morning, providing protection for what was described by Control as a 'Special Convoy'. It was difficult to determine why it has been so labelled as it consisted merely of one old rusty merchantman of about 2000 tons, escorted by two destroyers. Some wag suggested it could have been bringing in a fresh supply of cigars for the Prime Minister! In the meanwhile, Pat Lyall had been at it again when he encountered a Ju 88 over the Isle of Wight and saw it off with one engine on fire. He is being allowed a 'Probable' for it.

Airborne again in the afternoon, when I took a section to The Needles to intercept a raid approaching from the south. However the raid turned westwards before coming within our orbit and made for Bristol, when it was dealt with by squadrons from 10 Group.

We clocked up a further fifty hours today and the chaps are becoming noticeably weary. It is not unusual to find some of them fast asleep in hard backed chairs or, on other occasions, whilst lying on the floor. I think the fact that we have so little to show for our efforts makes it seem all the more tiring.

Archie McKellar has just been on the phone with the sad news that his CO, Walter Churchill, has been killed. It is an ill wind however, for Archie has been given command of 605 Squadron and has also won a bar to his DFC.

27th September Findlay had a fine old battle over Southampton yesterday when he and his boys ran into a mixed bag of Do 17's and

Ju 88's. They accounted for four of the blighters, although two of our own machines returned with substantial cannon fire damage. Several other section patrols were flown throughout the day with no further interceptions being made. In fact, we must beware of allowing the patrols to seem routine, otherwise the boys will become careless. It is important that we don't relax, for familiarity fosters contempt, and that can be fatal at a time like this.

It has not gone unnoticed that Eddie always turns up for lunch whenever Pauline is on the waggon, and today was no exception. During the meal he insisted that Gini and I should join Pauline and him for dinner at The Spread Eagle, at Midhurst. Presumably he wanted adequate chaperonage! However, I was glad we went, for it is a super place; very Ye Olde Worlde; where the car park attendant performs his duty dressed in a suit of mediaeval armour incongruously bedaubed with red paint: where rows of little plum puddings hang from the rafters in the dining room ready to be eaten at Christmas, when they will be replaced by this year's vintage which will remain aloft for the next twelve months: where the food is excellent and mine host hospitable. Eddie paid the bill and the girls were impressed with the evening, as indeed was I. Doubtless his intentions are honourable!

With A Flight near Dungeness this morning when a number of 109's again bore down on us without warning. However, we were able to side-step them this time and Babbage actually fired at one before they all climbed away like bubbles in a bath. I don't think he connected, though. Jerry seems loath to mix it with us these days.

We had no further excitement today and I have been able to bring some of our records up-to-date. It is interesting to note that the Squadron bag is now 71 destroyed with a further 21 probably destroyed. On the debit side, we have lost twenty two aircraft and three pilots killed. Mind you, we have an advantage over the Germans for, when our lads bale out, they live to fight another day, whereas the Jerries go straight into the bag.

29th September Had a hairy experience yesterday morning when my undercarriage jammed after patrolling with 213 Squadron. It had been an uninteresting patrol, stooging backwards and forwards between Beachy Head and Dungeness for an hour without seeing any action and, when I selected 'Wheels Down' after joining the circuit, both warning lights remained red. Opened up to overshoot and called Pedro to fly alongside to have a look at the wheels, when he reported one leg appeared to be down but that the other had barely freed itself from the wing faring. So we cleared from the circuit while I set about sorting out the problem.

I dived the aircraft steeply and tugged out of it, hoping to free the obstruction, repeating the manoeuvre several times, but Pedro reported no change. Resorted to using the emergency air bottle when there was a scrunch and a thud as one light changed to green while the other remained red. It may have looked pretty but, believe me, it is an alarming combination of colours. I don't think I have ever landed a Spitfire so gingerly but, more by luck than good guidance, everything held together and I was thankful to clamber out at dispersal. It turned out to be a leak in the hydraulic system.

We have reverted to Alert Two again. Hooray!

Am writing this at Lavington where I am staying for the weekend. Euan is not well and is remaining in bed. Barbie thinks he has been doing too much, which is probably so. After all, he stepped into the London Commissioner's job straight after being Minister of Transport, which, I should imagine, would be enough to tax even the hardiest of souls. David Margesson and Mrs Dudley Ward are also house guests, David taking a breather from the rigours of Parliament and the latter because she has been bombed out of her London home. I showed David round Westhampnett this afternoon as he is much interested in what we are doing.

30th September Returned early this morning as it was my day on stand-by, and found George Pinkerton had turned up while I had been at Lavington. George has been posted to Turnhouse as a Controller and is presently undergoing a course of training at Stanmore. It was good to see him again, although he must have thought me inhospitable as I was for ever having to dash off to fly.

Got involved in three sorties today. The first was a very short affair when we were ordered to land after only ten minutes in the air. The second merely found us interrogating one of our own

Blenheims. However, the third led us to a squadron of unescorted Ju 88's over Cowes. What a change! Only twelve of them. They scattered as soon as they spotted us diving on them from 15,000 feet but they were not quick enough. Managed to pick one out and gave it a five second burst, when the port engine exploded and the wing parted company with the fuselage. I only saw one fellow getting out as the Junkers disappeared below me in a series of flick rolls.

It was a satisfactory engagement from our point of view as we downed six and left two more limping towards France with smoke pouring from both engines.

Jack called up as I was changing to go out for dinner and asked me to look in at Tangmere on my way past as he had one of the Ju 88 pilots in the guard room who apparently wanted to meet one of his adversaries. I was curious when I entered and more than surprised to be confronted by a fresh faced youngster who could not have been more than eighteen years of age. He was very correct in manner, with clicking heels and all that, but the gist of the message I was given was that he wanted to hand over his Luger to me as a sort of trophy of war. Needless to say, I was pleased to have it, and even more pleased when he also presented me with his flying helmet, mae west, and the orange coloured velvet scarf he has been wearing.

Gini and I reached Arundel without mishap this time, although my encounter with Fritzie had made us late arriving. However our host and hostess were very understanding and we spent a most enjoyable evening at the castle. After dinner Bernard introduced me to a new game he says he invented. It consists of slinging billard balls at one another across a billiard table, although I never quite cottoned to the reason for doing it. Bernard calls the game Billiards Fives. I call it bloody murder! I can hardly hold a pen now!

Message from Eddie waiting for me when I got back. He and Pauline have just announced their engagement!

October

1st October Mickey was a bit off colour this morning so I offered to stand in for him, at the same time hoping that Jerry would follow his recent pattern of leaving us alone during the mornings because I had invited the Duke of Norfolk to pay us a visit. Of course, Jerry did not oblige and the Squadron was scrambled soon after the Duke arrived. However Gini had turned up with her waggon by this time and I was able to leave Bernard in her care whilst I attended to matters aloft.

We were ordered to the Isle of Wight to intercept an incoming raid at Angels 15 and got into position in double quick time. There was much broken cloud in the area and we were nearly taken by surprise when a number of 109's jumped us from behind a cloud, but Paddy Barthropp saw them coming and gave us a chance to dodge them. As a matter of fact, I was a little apprehensive as we had five new boys with us, but I needn't have worried, for they all acquitted themselves admirably. In fact John Willie Hopkins lost his combat virginity in the brief engagement which followed and managed to get in a burst on one of the Messerschmitts before it disappeared again, but I don't think he hit it. Nevertheless, it was a beginning for him and he will have plenty more opportunities in the future. No one else managed to get a shot in, for the 109's pulled away as soon as they had made their thrust and easily outpaced us in the climb. I think they were some of the new 109E's. No one reported any damage, so we reformed over Portsmouth and continued the patrol.

Control then told us there was a battle going on over The Needles, so we went there, but saw no signs of any conflict – only an empty sky. I expect it was just our own plots becoming confused again. At any rate, we were told to pancake soon after when I found Bernard still propped up against the side of the tea waggon drinking his third cup of Virginia's coffee. He invited me to a cocktail party at Arundel and asked me to give a lift to the guests from Lavington as Barbie had apparently used up her monthly ration of petrol coupons.

There is only one bath in the farmhouse so, in order to save both time and hot water, we normally get into it three at a time, sitting side-on with our legs dangling over the edge. We have had constructed a long board which fits lengthwise on top of the bath and this serves as a table for the pre-prandial drinks which Mr Motto brings in on a tray. Findlay came across him this evening, standing outside the bathroom door with a tray of drinks in one hand and a stopwatch in the other.

'What the hell are you doing there, Mr M?' asked Findlay. 'The CO told me to bring the same again in five minutes time', he replied, 'but there are still thirty seconds to go!' I don't know what we would do without Mr Motto!

Duly carried out my duties as chauffeur and was liberally entertained at the castle before returning to Lavington for dinner. A lone raider came over while we were at table and dropped a couple of bombs in the Park which brought down two large pine trees and cracked a number of windows in the house. We later found a large concrete ornamental jar had been smashed on the patio outside, spilling earth and plants all over the place.

2nd October Findlay was at the sharp end this morning, so I was able to entertain Willie Nicholson of the 16th Lancers whom I had invited to come along at the party last night. It is good to see fellows from the other services, taking an interest and Willie has promised to give me a ride in one of his tanks sometime soon. Green Section took off while he was with us and Findlay and Barthropp clobbered a Ju 88 just off the coast. That notches up Boyd's twelfth victory so it will be interesting to see whether the gong rationing system will work in his case.

I may be wrong, but things seem to be easing off a bit these days, and most of our recent interceptions have been of singleton aircraft, but more often we only spot 109's cruising around at heights well above 30,000 feet. These occasionally make furtive darts at us before soaring up again to their superior position, where they seem content to sit in a kind of haughty dignity, no doubt consuming large quantities of oxygen while doing so.

We gather the boys at Biggin Hill are finding the same thing and certainly we are not being sent into their area so often now. In fact, this sense of relaxation even seems to be permeating into the lives of the local civilians, for hardly an evening now goes by without some of us being asked out. Everyone is really most hospitable around these parts. Indeed Jack and I were invited to Lavington this evening when we must have been the only two whose names did not appear in *Who's Who!* Bernard and Lavinia Norfolk, John and Anne Cowdray, Davina Erne, Johnny Wallace and Gini, together with our hostess, made up the dinner table. Euan was there to begin with but excused himself before we sat down to our meal. He does not look at all well.

I later drove Jack back to Tangmere, calling at the Operations Room on the way. The plotting table was devoid of plots, apart from a few showing that London was still having its nightly visitation. Could it be that the Germans have had enough?

4th October The glass has been falling and it has rained continuously since yesterday morning. It is almost like a Scotch mist heavily watered down and Findlay took off to test conditions, but came straight in off the circuit because he found he was in cloud well below two hundred feet!

Bernard took me to meet the Chief Constable this morning as I wanted to ask him if it would be possible to close the road to the public, as it is posing a continual threat to our security, especially since our Bessoneau hangar has gone up in the field on the opposite side of the road from the flying field. As I explained to him, we spend a lot of time moving sightseers away from the area when the lads could be more gainfully employed elsewhere. However, one we just cannot budge. Mrs Sprague. The poor soul sits in her car for hours just gazing towards the B Flight huts as if willing her husband to walk through the door. It is really tragic for all of us, for there is still no news of her husband, and we fear he must have come down in the sea. Nor is there any news of Harry Moody, whose brother had also been in touch with me. Alas, I can offer neither much comfort and I find the whole thing deeply distressing. However Ralph Hubbard has come up trumps again and has offered to let us have another barn to replace A Flight's marquee which is leaking like a sieve.

Had a rough time at Arundel this evening! It started with drinks in the Lancers' Mess, followed by dinner with the Norfolks, but this ended up with an inevitable game of Bernard's billiards fives, during which a ball went through a window and I had the shirt ripped off my back by the noble Duke trying to prevent a goal being scored! As I complained to him at the time, it was no way for the Earl Marshal to behave! This morning did not start very well either, as I missed breakfast and now heard that Gini's van has broken down near Boxgrove!

5th October The weather has cleared at last and it was a relief to get into the air again, when I led two patrols this morning. However, I could find no trade. Mickey and Pedro had better luck in the afternoon when they caught up with a Ju 88 as it was clearing the Isle of Wight. They got within firing range as it neared the French coast and left it diving towards Boulogne with one of its engines on fire.

Gini and Diana Duff-Cooper were on the waggon today and joined us for a ringside view of 609 Squadron in action when they waded into a formation of 109's near Middle Wallop. The action happened very high up and well to the west of us, but strangely enough it was the first time I had ever watched a dog fight from the ground, and I thoroughly enjoyed the experience, particularly as 609 did so well and brought down a number of the enemy. We could see three Messerschmitts spinning out of control at one time and it was encouraging to notice that all the Spitfires were still flying when the action finally disappeared from view.

We had another surprise visit from a low flying Ju 88 this evening, but our Bofors gunners were awake this time and soon had the air around us filled with brightly coloured flaming balls, which swished over our heads from all points of the compass. The guns from Tangmere joined in and, between them they put on a first class fireworks display, the choomph choomph of the Bofors mingling with the staccato barking of the light machine guns. Flaming tracers seemed to be going everywhere except into the Ju 88, which disappeared rapidly into a cloud! It had been a spectacular, but lethal, display! However there were no reports of bombs being dropped.

Sir Cyril Newall has been appointed Governor General of New Zealand, which is a very nice honour for the RAF. Sir Charles Portal has become Chief of the Air Staff in his place.

7th October Findlay has gone off on well-earned leave and Donald has just got back from his. He reports that Glasgow is peaceful and he very decently called to see Margaret while he was up north and says she is well.

The AOC 11 Group called on us today and this was the first time I had met Keith Park, the tall New Zealander who flies himself around in a Hurricane wherever he goes. I was invited to lunch with him at Tangmere, during which he disclosed the information that the Germans are now using some of their fighters to drop bombs. They must surely be very tiny bombs! At any rate we will look out for them from now on.

Got involved in an incident-packed patrol this afternoon which started off in company with 607 and 213 Squadrons as we climbed towards the west. Just as we were getting into the top cover position I noticed Vick's two weavers colliding and both aircraft spinning into the ground, when only one parachute was seen to open. However we continued to Portland and circled Weymouth without meeting any bandits. We were then ordered back to Southampton, but saw nothing there either. Finally, a solitary plot popped up near Brighton, when I detached Blue Section, consisting of Donald and Sergeant Whall, to deal with it whilst the rest of us returned to base. During the ensuing action Donald and Whall shot down a Do 17 after which they, too, turned for home. But something very strange happened. According to Donald, he and Whall were flying along together in a loose formation when, without any warning at all, Whall suddenly peeled way from him and flew straight into the ground near Arundel. The cause of the accident is a complete mystery unless, of course, a bullet had nicked one of the control wires which suddenly snapped in flight. But Donald says he did not see any return fire coming from the Dornier and Whall had given him no indication that anything was amiss.

Took up one further patrol this evening which was pancaked after being airborne for less than fifteen minutes. Eddie threw a party in The Ship afterwards to celebrate his engagement, when Trevor and Nanki did us proud.

9th October Autumnal weather is setting in and we have experienced its full range during the past couple of days, from low clouds and rain yesterday to a full gale today! I flew a weather test this morning, and although conditions showed signs of clearing in the West, it is real Harry Clampers stuff in the other direction. However, the so-called ill wind brought with it a very pleasant surprise in the shape of Archie McKellar who lobbed into Westhampnett because the weather was too bad for him to get back to his own base, Croydon. It was great to see him again and he seems to be doing as well as ever and relishing the job of running 605. He himself accounted for five 109's on Monday! But he says it is hard going having to operate from the London area because they get so little sleep because of the continual bombing, and I must admit he was looking weary. We are luckier in this part of the Sector and I tried to persuade him to doss down here for the night, but the weather cleared and he had to go.

As a matter of fact, 602 had to go too when a sizeable raid sprang up over Southampton, but the boys lost track of it in the heavy cloud. I was not flying on this sortie and, as I stood near the dispersal waiting for the lads to come back, was aware of a salvo of bombs bursting ever closer to the airfield as a low flying Ju 88 emerged from a cloud over the far corner. It is really extraordinary how like a Blenheim it looked!

However none of us waited long to examine the similarity for we realised Jerry was also blazing away with his fore and aft guns and dashed for cover instead! He flashed overhead in the direction of Tangmere, hotly pursued by the brightly coloured balls as the Bofors came alive again. Peeping out from behind my tree, I was in time to see two more bombs leaving the aircraft, presumably aimed at Tangmere itself, and listened while they exploded on impact. By some miracle, nothing was hit, but it was a damned impudent raid and one could almost imagine Jerry putting his fingers to his nose as he whizzed over our heads. I didn't see that, of course. I was too busy cowering behind a tree!

I took the next patrol myself when the squadron was sent to Brighton to try to deal with some 109's which were apparently making a nuisance of themselves with their little bombs. However they had left before we got there, so we still have to see this new breed of German for ourselves. The weather was still lousy in the area and I nearly couped J on its nose when landing. The wind was blowing at over 40 knots at the time.

The domestic side has not been without incident either as I had to call to see Daddy Drudge this morning to straighten out a matter of unpaid mess bills. He says our lads are bad settlers and I can see I will have to read the riot act to them!

11th October Have almost lost count of the number of Sections sent off today, but none had any successes to report. Mind you, the weather is bad and it is obviously affecting the enemy as well as ourselves, because he has become very circumspect about calling on us and only turns up one at a time, or occasionally as a pair – and these are usually just 109's. However London is still being thumped every night and I took Donald and Mac to positions over Hastings at dusk hoping to intercept some of the early marauders, but we had no luck. It was dark by the time we returned to base so Mac and Donald put down at Tangmere where the flare path was lit. However, I thought I would have a go at getting back into

Westhampnett, so latched on to the Chichester road which I could identify by the number of car headlights on it and flew up it until reaching the Westerton crossing, when I switched on my landing light, turned left and scraped into Westhampnett by the skin of my teeth! Having nearly rammed the A Flight dispersal hut, I don't think I will try that Smart Alec trick again!

The squadron collected more gongs today when Findlay's bar came through and Cyril Babbage was awarded a DFM. However, we have sad news too, for Sergeant Sprague's body has just been washed up on the beach at Brighton, having been missing for the past three weeks.

13th October Even the Controllers at Group are now grumbling that they have not seen a decent raid for weeks! All they have had to contend with has been a number of nuisance attacks by fighters carrying bombs, and these are like dealing with annoying pests which are difficult to get rid of. The boys got among some today but the result was indeterminate from our point of view, although encouraging from theirs. Babbage was shot down at Lewes, although himself uninjured, and Hart returned with category two damage to his aircraft. However the boys later made amends and saw off a Ju 88 in mid Channel.

A past CO of 603 Squadron, Count Stevens, has recently become the Station Commander at Ford and he flew over to see me today, saying he wanted to show off his new toy! This turned out to be an American Boston aircraft which had been built for the French Air Force and therefore had everything written on it in French. Count wanted to take me for a flight but, having forgotten to bring with him the pilot's notes and not being too familiar with the language, he succeeded instead in setting one of the engines on fire while starting up! That put an effective kibosh on my trip and he had to abandon the aeroplane at Westhampnett, where it is still sitting up on its tricycle undercarriage looking for all the world like a broody hen, and return to his own station by road. Count said he would send a ground party to repair the damage later.

Jack and I dined with David Niven at The Ship this evening. He tells us he has been inveigled into the Public Relations field where he is to make a new film. Well well, some people can have it with jam on both sides!

14th October I had gone over to Tangmere this morning to make arrangements for Sergeant Sprague's funeral when I was told that B Flight had been scrambled from Westhampnett, in spite of my instructions that the aircraft were to be kept on the ground on account of the appalling weather. So I left Crackers to get on with the funeral details and rushed over to the Operations Room to find a new officer on duty, someone I had never met before. Doubtless he had only been trying to impress his new masters. Be that as it may, it certainly failed to impress me! He had originally ordered the lads to climb above the clouds to investigate an unidentified plot, but when I entered the Control Room, the section was still in the clag at 25,000 feet and Donald was reporting that it still looked mighty dark to him!

I am afraid I broke the rules and insisted on taking over control of the Flight, as I knew Donald had two of our less experienced chaps with him. Fortunately the plots of the fighters were coming in clearly so I was able to direct the Flight over the sea and let it down gently until they ultimately broke clear, by which time they were well below a thousand feet! Hardly the sort of weather for inexperienced pilots to be flying in, especially under the guidance of an equally inexperienced controller!

Merston is the other satellite airfield in the Tangmere Sector and it lies some miles to the south and west of the main base, between Tangmere and Bognor Regis. It has not been occupied so far, but Jack decided it was time he put one of his squadrons into it. So Stuart Macdonald was bidden to move 213 Squadron this afternoon. I was still at Tangmere after ensuring our lads had all landed safely, when Mac told me of Jack's plans to move his squadron, and I was curious to find out how they would fare, as one of our lads had passed by Merston recently and had mentioned that it looked awfully soft. I therefore waited until 213 took off and followed them over in my car, when I arrived later at Merston to find seven Hurricanes scattered around the field, up to their armpits in mud! The ground was like a dish of freshly boiled toffee and it appears that someone has forgotten to put in the drainage! I left Mac to it, but I am told Jack has now had second thoughts about the wisdom of the move and 213 is back at Tangmere, at least for the time being.

Douglo Hamilton turned up unexpectedly this afternoon, saying he would like to spend the night. This was slightly awkward for me as I had been invited to dine at Arundel Castle. However, when I telephoned Bernard to explain my predicament, Douglo was immediately included in the invitation, and we were able to spend a delightful evening in each other's company after all. Strangely enough, it was the first time the two premier dukes had met one another!

15th October Just after Douglo left by car to pick up his aeroplane at Kenley, the squadron was scrambled to patrol Portsmouth–Southampton at Angels 25. Arriving at the position we could see the enemy trails well above us, so decided to climb after them in a fit of enthusiasm. Fortunately our quarry had gone by the time we reached the trails at 34,000 feet for our Spitfires were literally hanging on the ends of their props at that height and we could have been in trouble if we had to do any violent manoeuvring. We struck a lot of ice on the way down and I could have done with one of our ki-gas arrangements!

As it was, thick frost formed both outside and inside the windscreens, making it difficult for the lads to keep station in the formation. I tried opening the hood, but it was much too cold to stick one's face over the side and had to settle instead for a descent on instruments when the frost melted in the warmer air.

Jack called a conference this evening at which he and his three squadron commanders discussed the problem of how to deal with the high-flying Messerschmitts. I think we have reached a sensible decision, which is to leave alone anything flying above 27,000 feet, on the grounds that the fighters could not operate at that height when carrying bombs, and those not carrying bombs were not doing any harm anyway. We are able to mix it with the 109's at lower altitudes. We later repaired to The Ship to join Findlay who was throwing a small party to celebrate his latest gong.

There was a full moon earlier tonight and the visibility was excellent. Am glad to say our night fighter Blenheims cashed in on it and shot down a Heinkel.

18th October Things have been ominously quiet for the past few days and we are beginning to wonder what Jerry is cooking up for us. On the few patrols we have carried out, ice trails high above us have been all we have seen, and whatever has been up there has either failed to spot us or has decided to ignore us completely, as they have not even bothered to come down and take a sniff. At any rate we have made no interceptions at all, which is not doing much for our Squadron bag!

A heavy mist came down while I was dining at Midhurst last night and I nearly collided with one of John Cowdray's deers when driving back through the park!

20th October Have just spent the week end in considerable comfort at Lavington. Poor Euan is confined to his bed, but as usual the house was full of guests. I have suggested to Barbie that she re-names her house Euston Station! John de Bendern was among the house party, but I remembered him better as John de Forest when he used to do so well as an amateur golfer. Known to his friends as Shrubbery, of course! However I had not appreciated that he was a Prince of Lichtenstein, so I will have to treat him with more respect from now on!

At all events, a few of us went to Windsor on Saturday to pick up two of the Wallace boys who are at school there and, having met them at The Burning Bush, took them to the Hind's Head at Bray for lunch. We made our first mistake here, for the boys spurned our offer of ginger pop and preferred to drink Pimm's No 1 Cup!

Then, after a most unsuitable lunch for a couple of growing lads, we perpetrated our second error by taking them to a local picture house which was showing a rather sexy film, in the middle of which Wallace Minor took ill and we only managed to get him outside in time! It was possible the Pimms, but it could equally well have been the film, for neither was very suitable for an impressionable schoolboy! All in all, we were glad to hand them back to the spartan care of their housemaster in the evening and get back to Lavington.

Shrubbery decided he needed exercise on Sunday morning and persuaded me to accompany him on a long walk over The Downs, where there are so many bomb craters that one could almost imagine one was walking on the moon! However, Eddie and Pauline joined us in the evening when we dined at The Ship. For some inexplicable reason we were invited to join a party of complete strangers who were apparently celebrating some girl's birthday!

21st October I wish I knew who had been responsible for my hangover, for I feel I ought to write and thank her for the party! It was hardly the best time to be feeling under the weather either, as I have been sitting all morning having my portrait drawn by Cuthbert Orde, an official war artist, who has been commissioned by The Air Ministry to do sketches of some of the fighter pilots, mine among them. However, neither of us liked the finished product and Turps Orde says he will do it again later!

Most of us took part in a patrol today, generally in sections of two aircraft, when our targets have been the high flying marauders which we have left alone, or the low flying fighter bombers which we have failed to catch! However, although London is still receiving a lot of attention from the Luftwaffe during the hours of darkness, Bomber Command aircraft are now retaliating by dropping bombs on Berlin and as far afield as targets in Italy. It is an encouraging sign, and one wonders whether the tide may have turned in our favour.

I am looking forward to ten days' leave which is due to start on the 24th, as it is some time since I last saw Margaret. However I am embarrassed to hear from Birdie Saul that Glasgow Corporation is arranging a special lunch for me on the 26th, in recognition of our efforts in the South. Ten to one I will have to make a speech!

23rd October Becoming unsettled at the thought of getting away, although there is plenty going on to keep my mind occupied, even if it could hardly be called productive! I took Blue Section on a patrol this morning when we were ordered to go to 30,000 feet plus. Why I do not know, for we could have done little about it if anyone else had been there and all we got for our trouble was to get thoroughly chilled followed by the inevitable battle with freezing windscreens on the way down.

As Pauline was on the waggon today, Eddie came for lunch and later took me to Chichester to have a look at the new Sector Operations Room being built there. It will be more commodious than the present one, and less vulnerable too, as the building at Tangmere suffered a near miss during the attack in August when two enormous cracks appeared down its walls.

New R/T sets have been arriving to be fitted to our aircraft, but unfortunately the slings are still missing, so I will not be able to try them out before I go off on leave. The sets are crystalised on a Very High Frequency band and they say it cuts out interference and that it is just like talking on a telephone.

Spent the evening at Lavington helping Gini and Barbie to straighten out their canteen books, when it seemed to me that the YMCA is not doing very well out of us! Gini is driving to the Midlands tomorrow and has offered to give me a lift as far as Birmingham, where I can pick up the night train, and thus miss the discomfort of the nightly raids on London.

24th October After I had handed over to Findlay, Mickey drove me to Lavington where I changed over to Virginia's little Morris eight for the onward journey. We stopped at Chiddingfold for lunch and at Stratford upon Avon for tea before going on to Birmingham where I was dropped at New Street Station. As the train was not due to leave until 9.30, I decided to have a meal in the Queen's Hotel.

The dining room was quiet when I went in, the only other patrons being an elderly couple seated at the far end of the room and a RN Lieutenant Commander at the next table to mine. A three-piece orchestra was busily scraping out melodies from *The Maid of the Mountains* and I thought how pleasant it would be to indulge myself a little by ordering, first some smoked salmon, followed by a nice juicy steak, medium rare. Shortly after giving my order, the sirens sounded and the noise of gunfire could be heard in the distance.

Was half way through the smoked salmon when a bomb struck the hotel. Oddly enough, it was difficult to realise what had happened at first, for the noise was just like someone slamming a door. Just a loud wallop, when my mind seemed to freeze momentarily as I mentally photographed the scene. A waiter who had been bearing aloft a large tray seemed to have disappeared, leaving his tray suspended in mid air like an object subjected to levitation. The orchestra had also disappeared, its three members having dropped their instruments as they dived beneath the grand piano. I remember exchanging glances with my Naval colleague, both of us briefly having stopped in mid bite. Then the full impact was upon us.

The large plate glass windows crashed to the floor, the service doors swung violently open and the head waiter, followed by a blast of dust laden air, was propelled into the room as if driven by an invisible hand. The poor chap was covered from head to foot in dust and rubble and was waving his hands above his head, all the while shouting 'Help!' at the top of his voice, whereupon we ran into the kitchens where a horrible sight met our eyes. The whole place was full of smoke and steam from overturned cooking vessels and pots, pans, grills and broken crockery lay strewn about the floor. Two white coated chefs lay half buried beneath the fallen rubble, whilst a third was pinned by a large chunk of masonry to the top of a hot plate. We managed to prise this poor fellow loose by putting our shoulders against the bricks and beams to free him and mercifully he was unconscious when we lifted him down.

A frantic clanging of bells heralded the arrival of the fire services and the room was soon swarming with firemen and blue helmeted rescuers, at which point the Navy and I were glad to retire from the ghastly sights. We introduced ourselves.

'Tommy Woodroffe', he announced.

Where, I thought, had I heared that name?

'BBC', he added.

Ah yes, that was it – 'The Fleet's Lit up!' We agreed to team up from then on.

We were told that help was needed on the roof, so ran upstairs as quickly as possible. The lifts were out of action. The section we reached was strewn with incendiary bombs spluttering and sizzling about us, on to which we poured the contents of every sand bucket in sight. I even wielded a stirrup pump for the first time in my life, and to some effect too, for we soon had all the fires out on our bit of roof. Mind you, I don't know what those below thought of us for shovelling incendiaries over the side of the building! We returned to ground level to take stock of the position and found the rescue services in full control.

So we stood outside for a few moments watching Marshall and Snelgrove's store opposite blazing furiously from top to bottom. The firm had been in the course of putting additional floors on its building and a large crane stood on the top, some six or seven storeys above ground level. When the flames reached it, the crane toppled over and crashed through the blazing building, sending up myriads of huge sparks and stoking the fires to such an extent that Tommy and I were driven indoors by the intense heat. We agreed it was the best display of fireworks either of us had seen. Even better than Spithead, said Woodroffe, but I forebore to ask him if he could remember!

Having found a bar still operating in the basement and having swilled out some of the taste of smoke, we looked in at the station to enquire about getting a train out of the city. However, it was soon apparent that the LMS was not going to operate from there tonight, so we returned to the hotel to seek something to eat, for neither of us had had much dinner. Fortunately our friend the head waiter was still around and, having first apologised that no meals would be possible for the time being, wheeled over the best part of a side of smoked salmon and invited us to help ourselves. That, of course, set up a man's sized thirst, so it was fortunate that the bar hours were extended to cope with the emergency!

Have taken a room for the remainder of the night. The windows are mostly missing; in fact there is still a lot of glass lying about in odd corners, and I have to be careful where I tread! However, I feel dead beat and am about to turn in. What price Birmingham! I would have been just as well off travelling via London after all!

25th October Woke up with a throbbing head and was immediately

conscious of a strong smell of smouldering timber. Still no hot
meals being served, so had to settle for a do-it-yourself breakfast of
cornflakes and a cup of coffee. This was followed by an argument
with the management who insisted on charging the full rate for my
board. Good old LMS!

The streets outside were cordoned off whilst the rescue services
got on with their grim task of burrowing through heaps of rubble to
reach the victims still buried beneath it. There was an uncanny
stillness, broken only by an occasional shout or by the hollow-soun-
ding 'clunk' as another charred beam was pitched aside while the
workers tore into those awesome mounds in the hope of bringing
out alive the people trapped inside.

No trains were yet running from New Street Station and I was
advised to try Monument Lane instead, which I thought was
perhaps an unfortunate name in the circumstances! Nor were there
any buses or taxis in the district, so had no option but to hump my
bag along the deserted streets until I reached Broad Street where I
eventually came across a taxi. To my complete surprise, I ran into
Dunlop Urie and his wife Mary, who had just arrived off a train
from Torquay, where Dunlop had been convalescing during his
spell of sick leave.

The remainder of the journey is best forgotten, for the train we
ultimately caught was cold, filthy, without any form of catering on
it, and it stopped at every station along the route. We had to stand
in the corridor as far as Carlisle when we eventually managed to
secure a seat for Mary, and it had already taken five hours to reach
that far! It was midnight before we pulled in to Central Station, by
which time the last tramcar had gone and it was a case of seeking
out one of the few taxis which had not already used up its ration of
petrol for the day. Nevertheless it was all well worth the discomfort,
for Margaret looked great!

26th October Not unexpectedly, I slept in this morning and ended up
with a frantic rush to get ready for the luncheon in the City
Chambers. However, all was well, and I was greeted most cordially
by The Lord Provost, Mr Dollan, for long a kenspeckle figure in
Glasgow and an erstwhile Labour militant who has mellowed con-

siderably under the responsibilities of his lofty appointment. In fact, he treated me as if I was his long lost son!

The 'Top Table' consisted of a number of senior officers, among them Birdie Saul, and I was surprised to find that well-known author J. B. Priestley also among the guests. We foregathered in the Lord Provost's private room before lunch where the City Officer, Tom Wilson, was commendably heavy handed when pouring out the drinks! It was an excellent lunch, after which flattering speeches were made by the Lord Provost and Mr Priestley, but I honestly cannot remember what nonsense I spoke in reply. At all events, the guests applauded politely and I got the impression that the City appreciated what we have been doing and I am sure the lads will be delighted when I tell them all about it.

The remainder of the day passed quickly, as a party of us went on to Shawfield Park in the afternoon to watch a football match between The Army and a team from the Norwegian Army, at which I sat next to Prince Olaf, who has a voice to match that of Padre Sutherland. At least it was through no lack of verbal support from their Crown Prince that the visitors were beaten! After taking tea with the players, I took Birdie to meet my parents, when Dad somehow managed to mislay the cork from the whisky bottle, after which Birdie deemed it wiser to stay the night in Glasgow!

29th October Am only now beginning to feel the benefit of my leave and had not before appreciated how tensed up I had become, although the sound of a telephone ringing still has me jumping out of my seat. I suppose this is only to be expected for, after all, we have been living at the end of one for so long, expecting an order to scramble.

Birdie returned to Gullane on Sunday and, after attending to a number of personal matters on Monday morning, called at the TA Headquarters to meet the Chairman, Colonel Leslie, who has kindly offered the Association's help to run my Squadron Benevolent Fund which, thanks to Mr Dollan's intervention, has now amassed a sum of money large enough to require expert management.

Had a surprise visit from Paul Webb yesterday evening, for I had not realised he was in Glasgow. I thought he was still convalescing in the South. He had apparently read in the newspapers that I was in town and took the trouble to come over to see me. He is looking fine now and is able to waggle his fingers again and says he hopes to rejoin us soon. Funnily enough, a telegram arrived from Crackers while he was in the house to say that 602, with Mickey at the helm had shot down eight Huns with no loss to themselves. It seems they are doing better without me!

And so to Uplawmoor, where we found Jean and Archie as conscientious as ever about their ARP duties. Archie is a warden whilst Jean takes her turn manning the telephone switchboard. In fact, they left Margaret and me to our own devices while they went off to do their spell on duty, Jean with her tea cosy tucked under her arm in case of trouble! Margaret and I managed to complete the Glasgow Herald crossword puzzle in their absence!

30th October Early morning sickness, which usually only portends one thing! However, we are both thrilled by the news that a baby is due next April. The mother-to-be took full advantage of her new-found status and remained in bed all morning. So, having fixed a compass rose on Archie's ARP map to help him with his plane spotting, and later completing the crossword puzzle for the second day running, finally talked Margaret into getting up and dressed before taking her to Glasgow to join Dunlop and Mary for dinner. There was another telegram from Crackers to tell me that the boys have clobbered yet two more 109's but that Sergeant Elcome is unfortunately missing from this action.

31st October Margaret and I were invited to a private lunch in the City Chambers today to which The Lord Provost had also invited Sir Hector and Lady Hetherington, the Principal and Vice-Chancellor of Glasgow University, in the course of which Mr Dollan asked me whether there was anything the lads really needed. I told him how generous everyone had already been supplying us with all sorts of comforts and jokingly added that the only thing we seemed to be without now were sheets! I thought no more about it, and later accompanied Paddy Dollan and his wife to Stobhill Hospital, where The Lord Provost opened a new biochemical research wing. We travelled to the ceremony in the Civic Rolls-Royce, which carries the unusual registration number G 0. While at Stobhill I was introduced to Fred Nancarrow, Air Correspondent of the *Glasgow Hearld,* who is anxious to write a story about 602 Squadron.

Had intended to spend a quiet evening with my parents this evening, but arrived at their flat to find Mother in the throes of a hen's bridge party and that Dad had rebelled and taken himself off to his club in self defence! I, too, made myself scarce.

November

1st November A Constitution was drawn up for the Squadron Fund at a meeting in the TA Headquarters this morning, as a result of which it now looks a most business-like affair! A permanent committee has been formed, with The Lord Provost as the ex-officio Chairman, the other members being The Deacon Convenor of the Trades, The Dean of Guild, The Officer Commanding No 602 Squadron together with Paddy Dollan and myself as Life Trustees of the Fund. Over £15,000 has already been collected, so it is just as well its management is being entrusted to such safe hands. Paddy Dollan and Dad joined me for lunch afterwards in the Royal Scottish Automobile Club where we bumped into Hector Maclean sporting a new tin leg. He seems to be coping with it very well indeed.

As my leave ends tomorrow I took Margaret and Ruth to the Alhambra theatre to see Ivor Novello in *The Dancing Years* this evening. It was a great show. An air raid alert sounded as we were coming out of the theatre, during which a thunderstorm broke out, when three balloons were struck by lightning and fell in flames. Everyone, including me, thought the Germans had come! However, the enjoyment of the evening was later marred when Crackers rang up to tell me that Archie McKellar had been killed in action. Apparently he was tangling with some 109's over Mayfield this morning when he was shot down. It is a hell of a loss, and I was reading about his award of a DSO only the other day. In fact, Archie has collected two DFC's and a DSO within the space of one month.

3rd November I suppose it was high time my leave was up, for the Lord Provost was beginning to treat me like a prize exhibit and was making a point of showing me off at every occasion, particularly when his own appearances had to do with war charities. Thus I accompanied him to inaugurate an exhibition in Blythswood Square yesterday morning when a captured Ju 88 was on display as the centre of the attraction. In the course of his speech Paddy spoke with pride of how this machine had been shot down by Glasgow's own squadron, although in truth I was tempted to point out that it would probably have had many more bullet holes in it if it had been! Never mind, many doubtless believed him, and it was all for a good cause. Besides he gave me a jolly good lunch afterwards!

Spent the afternoon saying farewell and packing my things and Dad stood me a taxi to the station when the time came to catch the night train. However I was very embarrassed to find a small reception party there to see me off, including The Lord Provost, the City Treasurer and the Chairman of Rangers Football Club, whilst Tom Wilson was standing near a luggage trolley loaded with parcels which, he told me, contained a quantity of bed linen for the lads in the Squadron. 'A small gift from The City of Glasgow', announced the LP 'with our compliments!'

As the train was late in starting, it could be reasonably explained by the guard mistaking the colour of my face for one of the signals set at red!

Somehow I can never master the ventilation system in a sleeping compartment, for I either get the thing going full toss, when the place resembles a tropical hothouse, or I go to the other extreme and end up with a blast of Arctic air whistling through the sleeper. I tried full heat with the window open, but the clickety-clack of the wheels nearly drove me bonkers! I was glad therefore, to stagger out at Euston after a sleepless night, to be met by Crackers who had driven up from Westhampnett to fetch me.

I have now resumed command from Findlay and have handed out the sheets. For that reason if for no other, the boys seem quite pleased to have me back!

5th November Am once again in harness and opted to lead the early patrol, for I not only wanted to get the feel of it again, but was anxious to try out the new VHF Radio, which turned out to be all it was cracked up to be, with practically no interference whatsoever, and all messages coming through loud and clear, strength nine! Also waded through the outstanding paper work which Crackers and Findlay had been unable to attend to.

Mr Motto has also been doing his stuff, for I found two floor rugs in my bedroom on my return together with a thoughtful vase of autumnal leaves on the chest of drawers. Wyer had been on leave at the same time as me and I was glad to hear that his house had escaped the bombing in Birmingham. He also expressed relief that no more cuspidors had been added to the inventory in his absence!

A lot of rain had fallen while I was away and the airfield is now very soft. Shades of Dyce! However I was only required to do one more sortie over the Isle of Wight, which incidentally turned out to be a false alarm, before being stood down for the night at six o'clock. It becomes dark early now.

Dined with Jack at Tangmere before going on to the WAAF quarters at Boxgrove where the girls were throwing a party. However we did not stay long, for both of us were tired and wanted an early night.

6th November Was busy dealing with a mountain of bumff in the office when a call came for the whole squadron to scramble, so I dropped everything and dashed off to lead it, since it was ages since we had had one of these! In the event, we intercepted about thirty bombed-up 109's approaching the Isle of Wight but, when they saw us approaching, they jettisoned their loads and scarpered, making no attempt to stay and fight it out. However I am pleased to say that McDowall got one as it scooted rapidly uphill. I saw it go down in flames. Some Hurricanes from Tangmere also arrived on the scene when Mac and one of the 213 boys were able to claim a second victory between them, but I did not witness that one as I was too busy trying to catch up with another 109 which was out-pacing me in the climb. Lord Trenchard had been right. The Germans *are* behaving just like a bunch of cissies!

Managed to get down in time to have a medical, not that I am unwell or anything like that. I am taking the precaution of keeping my Commerical Pilot's Licence valid in case the war should end and I want to go back into civil aviation assuming, of course, that there will still be civil aircraft for me to fly! I was passed fit in spite of the vicissitudes of ten days in Scotland!

Was ordered up again – in the middle of lunch, of course – when Nigel Rose and I found ourselves being vectored in and out of a mass of large billowy clouds somewhere over The Channel. Just as we were rounding a particularly large cumulus we suddenly found ourselves face to face with a Ju 88, when I don't know which of us was the more surprised. Perhaps it was Jerry, for he immediately pulled away, presenting us with a broadside target which we were not slow to exploit. I was able to get a short burst in on him when I saw the rear gunner slump forward and his gun point vertically up-wards before the aircraft found refuge in the next cloud. Intelligence are allowing a 'damaged' for it.

8th November Jerry has become more active in the dark recently and dropped a stick of incendiaries on the airfield last night, one of which burned brightly only yards from one of B Flight's Spitfires. Fortunately the duty guards were alive to the situation and dealt with it before it could do any damage, but they are a damned nuisance just the same as they all have to be swept up, otherwise they puncture the tyres when we run over them.

145 Squadron, whom we relieved at Westhampnett in August, is back at Tangmere to take over from 607 Squadron. We will miss Jimmy Vick and his boys, but it is good to see Johnny Peel again and to know that he has recovered from his injury. Dunlop Urie has also turned up and we have been pulling his leg that he only came back so that he could muscle in on Jack's party!

It is no secret that Jack does not like Germans, nor has he made any secret of the fact that he believes Hitler still intends to launch his invasion. That being so, he is determined that none of the hard earned funds of his Officers' Mess should be put at risk, and what better way of disposing of them, he reasoned, than to spend them all on one super party. Hence the occasion.

Anyone who ever had any connection with Tangmere seemed to be invited. The Commander-in-Chief, the AOC, the Under-Secretary of State, the Government Chief Whip, the Crazy Gang, the Windmill Girls, fellows from all the squadrons which had operated from the field, our friendly neighbours, Uncle Tom Cobley and All – they were there. So, having picked up a car load of guests from Lavington and driven them to Tangmere, we arrived to find the Mess in a turmoil, the building crammed with human beings, most of whom seemed to be either struggling to get into the bar or struggling to get out of it. There was standing room only in the corridors and everyone had to shout to be heard.

Nevertheless everyone appeared to be merry, and rumour had it that the first person to pass out was one of the waiters who was seen to keel over half an hour before the party was due to begin! Not surprisingly, the Crazy Gang failed to perform, but no one either cared nor noticed and, at one point in the evening, I saw Jimmy Nervo sitting in a corridor with a curvacious Windmill Girl on either side of him, whilst Teddy Knox was acting as an extra barman in company with Bud Flanagan. I am told it was a good party and, if my head this morning is anything to go by, I am sure I have been informed correctly! However I was somewhat worried when Harold Balfour rang to thank me for driving him and David back to Lavington after the show was over, for I have no recollection of going that far!

10th November Felt awful on the early patrol yesterday when we prayed hard that the Germans would not show up. Thank goodness our prayers were answered, a sentiment shared by Jack who came on the R/T to ask me how I was feeling. The sound of his voice was like a load of gravel being poured into our eardrums, for I don't think he had even been to his bed by then! Heaven protect us from the Social Whirl, for it is wreaking more damage than the Hun at the moment! And it did not end with Jack's party either. Gee Wallace is marrying Elizabeth Koch de Guyrend the day after tomorrow and we were invited to pre-nuptial drinks with them at Lavington this evening, having undergone a session with Dunlop Urie the night before. Sometime in between bouts, the Duke and Duchess of Richmond paid us a visit and one is beginning to wonder whether the war is still on!

12th November We had a Squadron photograph taken yesterday on the lawn in front of the farmhouse when the problem was to eject from the group a lot of hangers-on determined to get in on the act. Even Virginia managed to get her face into one shot when she looked out of a window in the background, requiring yet one more plate to be exposed! However, the dogs were allowed to remain!

The Squadron has not been called upon for the past two days and we are wondering whether the enemy has given us up as a bad job – or maybe as too good a job! At all events, we have been able to use the time for indulging in squadron formation practices and to teach the newer fellows some of the tricks to give them a better chance when they have to go into action. I always feel sorry for new lads when they find themselves early on having to master the intricacies of a Spitfire whilst tangling with an angry Messerschmitt at the same time. One at a time is enough! However, they are all coming along fine.

Elizabeth and Gee were married yesterday in Midhurst Register Office with a reception afterwards at Lavington, where I had the pleasure of meeting Barbie's parents, Sir Edwin and Lady Lutyens. Sir Edwin is a great old boy with a good eye for the girls, and sometime during the proceedings was caught pursuing one of the maids round the room, wearing a black homburg upside down on his head pretending, as he later explained, to be an unorthodox priest endeavouring to give the girl absolution! Alas, she proved to be too nimble for him! He is a great architect and has been responsible for designing many remarkable buildings as far apart as New Delhi in India and our own Waterloo Bridge in London. We have to thank him also for the many attractive RAF Stations which were built during the late thirties.

Douglas Farquhar chose to pay us a visit at the happy moment when we were about to celebrate Mickey's DFC at The Victoria. Everyone is delighted about the gong, for Mickey Mount is a most popular fellow. A bit of a stutterer at times perhaps, but one never hears it on the R/T – not even on the new VHF sets!

13th November Some have all the luck! I sat on readiness throughout the morning, and although sent off twice, have nothing to show for the effort. Then, no sooner had I handed over to Findlay when his Flight was ordered off and he shot down a Ju 88. Dunlop went with him on that sortie to have a last ride with the squadron before leaving to become an instructor at No 55 Operational Training Unit at Aston Down. I later received an irate telephone call from Johnny Peel, complaining that he had seen the Junkers first but that Findlay had nipped in ahead of him and deprived him of his spoils! They say all is fair in love and war!

Officialdom seems bent on getting our likenesses on canvas, for another war artist has turned up to paint our portraits. This time it is Olive Snell, and Mickey has been selected as her first model. Mickey himself is dubious about the undertaking in case the artist should want to portray him in classical form wearing nothing more than a protective fig leaf!

Ian Ferguson failed to regain his flying category and was recently appointed ADC to the Duke of Kent. He brought his new master to see us this evening when HRH stayed for supper. We had an interesting chat, mainly about London night clubs for some unknown reason, when The Prince admitted to having visited a few, although he says his mother does not approve! I can well imagine!

15th November We had a quiet day yesterday with nothing more exciting than a number of routine patrols to perform. However, an outbreak of sore throats and influenza has depleted our state and I have had to recall some chaps off leave. I am glad I have, for Jerry has woken up unexpectedly and has started to show some interest in us again.

I led the Squadron on three patrols today when German fighters were reported to be active over the South Coast. We saw nothing on

602 Squadron at Westhampnett, November 1940. Seated in the front row are F/L Mount, DFC, F/L Boyd, DFC, myself, S/L Urie and F/L Jack.

Myself at Prestwick in March 1941.

the first sortie and only a few 109's very high up on the second. However 213 Squadron and ourselves spotted a gaggle of enemy fighters at about 27,000 feet on the third occasion and were determined not to let them get away. All of us were so intent on concentrating on our prey ahead that none saw their chums swooshing down on us from behind, causing a real old ding-dong to start up, with tracers flying indiscriminately in all directions. They disappeared just as suddenly as they arrived. Just like that. The sky miraculously clear again. That's what happens. So we returned to base feeling rather sheepish, for none of us was able to file a claim. McDowall was even more despondent, for he got clobbered and had to make a wheels up landing at Birdham with some nasty shrapnel wounds in his face. I fear this affray has neither improved his looks, his temper – nor his language!

18th November It was only a flash in the pan, for the enemy must have gone back into hibernation. At least we have been left severely alone for the past three days. As a matter of fact, I am glad of the respite for we are still short of pilots, being now without Mac and Cyril Babbage, who is the latest victim of the flu bug. However, we have received posting notices for three new pilots, although none has yet shown up. There is news too of a second squadron coming to Westhampnett shortly and it is reported to be a Polish outfit. Jack says he will come over tomorrow to discuss the details with me.

   The Prime Minister has been saying nice things about us fighter boys in The House of Commons. He says we have just won a famous victory although, to be honest, I don't think any of us has been aware that there has been that sort of battle going on!

19th November Jack came over as promised this morning and told me that 302 (Polish) Squadron will be arriving on Saturday and where the hell was he going to put it! We are already overflowing our own restricted accommodation, so it looks very much as if the new arrivals will have to go under canvas on the far side of the airfield. I don't envy them, though, for the ground is very muddy at the moment, a fact which was amply demonstrated to Jack when Sergeant

Cordell, one of the three new lads who only joined us this morning, turned a Spitfire on its back on the completion of his first training flight with the Squadron. Some start for the poor fellow!

Geoffrey Quill flew in again with another modification for us to try out. This time it was a Spitfire fitted with metal ailerons which, when I flew the machine, turned out to be a big improvement over the fabric covered version. I found it to be much lighter and more positive on the controls. Findlay tried it out later and confirmed my opinion, so we have told Geoffrey we would like to buy some!

Someone discovered that Hilary Dale and his wife were on holiday nearby, so Findlay, Donald and I took our pre war Regular Adjutant for a night out at The Victoria. Our reunion was somewhat spoilt when a local tart, considerably inebriated, made a nuisance of herself by trying to latch on to our party. However, Findlay eventually slipped her a Mickey Finn when she passed out inside a nearby telephone booth. Even Hilda approved of the remedy, although it cost us the price of a taxi to take the trollop home!

20th November Mickey has gone with Olive Snell to have his portrait painted so I was standing in for him when A Flight was scrambled to St. Catherine's Point, where a Dornier had been reported overhead. However we saw nothing of it and returned to refuel but, before it was completed, the entire squadron was scrambled to go back to St. Catherine's at top speed. Once again we encountered nothing and A Flight was then ordered to land whilst B Flight remained on patrol. This time they encountered one of our own Blenheims, which seems to be an instance of slight over-reaction!

Since Mr Churchill spoke of us in such glowing terms last week, Spitfires have become 'de rigueur' nationwide and local communities throughout the county have been rapidly organising 'Spitfire Funds' as a means of raising money for the war effort. It was inevitable therefore that Barbie would be in the forefront of her local effort, so it was no surprise to be invited to appear at the function she organised in her nearby village of Graffham. It took the form of a dance in the local hall and it was well attended by everyone, the gentry conspicuous in their natty suitings while the

November   163

rest turned up sweaters, scarves and farm boots. Everyone mucked in together and everyone thoroughly enjoyed themselves. My job was to pick the winning ticket for the raffle, which resulted in the winner being presented with a bottle of Haig. Barbie tells me her little effort has netted a profit of £42.

23d November Torrential rain fell during the night and the airfield now resembles a lake, making it impossible to operate aircraft from it. I nearly tipped J on its nose when taxying to a drier spot, even with two fellows sitting on the tail to weight it down! Nevertheless we maintained a token state of two aircraft throughout, but luckily they were not called for, and Mickey was able to get away for a second sitting with Olive. He says it is all right and that he has not been asked to remove any clothing so far!

302 Squadron was due this morning but bad weather delayed their arrival until late afternoon, by which time Jack was just about having kittens. However they came in eventually and seem resigned to living rough in sodden tents. Rather them than me! Jack Satchell commands the unit. In fact he has been with it for some time and has already won the Polish equivalent of our Victoria Cross – The Vituti Militari I believe, although better known to our lads as the Tutti Frutti!

While Jack and I were talking to Satchell, our attention was drawn to a Spitfire making an awkward approach to the airfield. It turned out to be John Willie Hopkins who then had the effrontery to land the Spitfire plumb on top of mine which was parked outside my office! Both aircraft were written off in the accident and young Hopkins has incurred the grave displeasure of his Commanding officer, for I had got used to J which is one of our few aircraft fitted with metal ailerons. It is lucky for him I am spending the weekend at Lavington!

Euan was up and about, but looking poorly, and Barbie is clearly worried about his health. Diana and Duff Cooper were also staying for the week end, Duff having recently become Minister of Information. We played silly party games after dinner when Diana and I made an inspired team in 'Under The Spreading Chestnut Tree', but Duff declined to take part in it under the pretext that it would be unbecoming for a Minister of The Crown!

25th November Flight tested F as a possible replacement for J. It is not nearly so pleasant to fly as my old aircraft, but it will do, so I have left it with Connors to have the letter J painted on the sides. It is better to stick to the same identification letter, for it makes it that much easier for the boys to recognise who is boss in the air!

Barbie rang to say she is taking Euan to London tomorrow to see a specialist. She is obviously very worried about him and I sincerely hope the diagnosis is good.

27th November We did several Section patrols yesterday, when Babbage had a brush with a Ju 88 on one occasion, and was allowed a 'damaged' for it. However things have been quiet on the whole, and we have been able to continue with our training programme. I am very pleased with the progress of the new lads and it says much for the Spitfire that the tyros are finding them so easy to come to terms with. It really is a splendid aeroplane and I would not want to change it for anything else on the books.

Had a letter from Paddy Dollan asking me to write an Appreciation about Archie for publication in the Scottish newspapers. This I am pleased to do, but I am less happy about his additional request to supply him with a 'Message' for inclusion in a brochure being prepared for Glasgow's War Weapons Week. These things take time to prepare.

Bernard and Lavinia invited me to stay at Arundel last night when, for once, we had a peaceful evening and I was able to retain my shirt! Bernard's sister was the only other guest. However, the shenanigans continued this evening at Bosham when Eddie threw a party at The Ship to work off steam before his wedding on Saturday. John de Bendern stayed with us at the farmhouse afterwards.

28th November We were visited by the new C-in-C Fighter Command today, Air Marshal Sholto Douglas, who talked to us about the possibility of going on the offensive soon. This is good news, for it means the Top Brass must reckon we have licked the Germans in their attempt to knock out our fighter defences. He added, however, that we would have to wait a little longer in order to build up our strength before committing Spitfires and Hurricanes over the Continent. Sir Sholto also asked for our views on a controversy which has been raging between the AOC's of 11 and 12 Groups as to whether it is better to operate our fighters in small units, which is the 11 Group thinking, or to wait until several Wings of fighters have formed up and then attack in strength, as the AOC 12 Group advocates. My own view is that we would seldom have enough time to wait for formations to form up. In any case, it has been my experience that formations get hopelessly split up anyway as soon as we go into action. The C-in-C was non committal on the matter! They say Stuffy Dowding will be retiring soon from the RAF and that he was due to leave in any case shortly after the war began. By Jove, it is fortunate for us he was allowed to stay on, for one has been conscious of a firm hand being at the tiller during the past few months.

While the C-in-C was with us, Mickey took the squadron on patrol to tackle a raid approaching the Isle of Wight very high up. I don't know whether the Ops people were merely trying to impress our distinguished visitor, or whether they had had a sudden rush of blood to the head, but the lads were ordered to 33,000 feet where they were well and truly outmanoeuvred by the 109E's. Pat Lyall was shot up but managed to keep up with the others on the return journey for most of the way when, for some inexplicable reason he baled out at low level, when his parachute failed to open. What rotten luck. The remainder returned to base in due course, but several aircraft required patching up.

30th November There was a blazing row about Thursday's action and Jack has been under pressure from Stuart Macdonald, Johnny Peel and myself to find out why, in the name of goodness, the boys were ordered to go so high, contrary to what we had all agreed previously. Jack's defence was that Mickey should have ignored the instruction but, when we pointed out that we would soon be up the creek without a paddle if everyone started to disobey orders, the Controller responsible was marched in and given an almighty dressing down in front of the three of us. I suppose there is no good crying over spilt milk, but it seemed pretty poor consolation for the loss of such a splendid chap.

However all roads led to Eddie's wedding on Friday and a number of us drove to Maidstone to position nearby for the ceremony next day. We chose to stay at The Star Hotel which must have been the coldest hostelry in England last night! Brass monkeys wouldn't have had a look in! However we met up with many chums who were foregathering for the fray, largely from Eddie's old squadron, 601. We later had to contend with the noise of a continual stream of Nazi bombers passing overhead, as well as the cold, and altogether had a somewhat disturbed night, especially as we heard several bombs dropping close by. Indeed, we were very nearly late for the service, for an unexploded bomb blocked our route and we had to make a lengthy diversion to get to the church on time. As it was, we just managed to squeeze into the very back pew. But Pauline looked lovely. Eddie just looked apprehensive!

The reception was held at the bride's mother's home, Leeds Castle, which is about the only castle remaining in the country with a fully serviceable moat running round it. I must say, it crossed my mind at the time that it was a mercy I had not been faced with a similar situation at my own wedding! It had been bad enough being perched on the top of a taxi! At the function itself I could not understand why the girls seemed to be curtseying left, right and centre until I realised the Duke of Kent was among the guests. He gave me a wink as he went by!

December

2nd December I am annoyed with the NAAFI for, until now, they have not been much in evidence and we never saw them during the months when we were under threat of constant air attack, during which time seldom a day went by when our dependable YMCA waggon did not turn up. And now the NAAFI is claiming its right of monopoly at all service establishments to have Gini's van barred from the airfield. Everyone I have spoken to has been sympathetic, but reckons there is not much that can be done about it, as NAAFI does indeed have the monopoly. Rights be damned, I say, and have written a letter to the US of S who has promised to look into the matter. I hope he manages to fix it, for the troops will play merry hell if our faithful waggon disappears from the scene! Have told Gini to carry on as usual and said that I will answer for the consequences! In fact, Gini brought her parents to visit us yesterday, when they stayed to tea. Mr Motto turned up trumps again on this occasion by appearing in a pair of white gloves!

We seldom see Germans in daylight nowadays and have been filling in most of our time practising attack procedures, sometimes in squadron strength against 65 Squadron which has recently taken over from 213, and who welcome this form of practice. Macdonald has taken 213 Squadron to Leconfield.

Olive Snell invited me to tea at her house in West Ashling to show her finished portrait of Mickey to me. It is good, and she now wants to start one of me and suggests we get on with it whilst things are relatively quiet.

Her husband, Colonel Pike, runs The Home Guard in the area. Olive paints under her maiden name.

Roddy McDowall has won a bar to his DFM.

5th December Most duty hours have been spent sitting at readiness in the crew room, because the weather has not been good enough for practice flying. Consequently I am becoming a dab hand at Ludo and am already 6d up in the series! However, I have taken over a new Spitfire fitted with metal ailerons and I gave it an air test yesterday. It was all right until landing, when the machine bounced a mile into the air as if propelled from a springboard. It later transpired there was too much fluid in the oleo legs.

Henry Grazebrook has been posted to Hornchurch on Administrative Duties. We are sorry to see him go, for he has done a first rate job with us as Intelligence Officer.

Olive began the portrait this morning with a sitting at Goodwood Dower House, where she has her studio. It is a strange building, completely round, and the first house I have been in which boasts a two-seater loo! Apparently the house was built by a past Duke of Richmond who, I reckon, must have been very much in love with his partner! They must have been sturdy characters too, for it is also one of the coldest houses I have ever been in! I hope Olive will allow herself some artistic licence when she comes to paint my nose, for it was decidedly blue in colour in these arctic surroundings!

Took Gini and Davina Erne to the Spread Eagle this evening. I suppose the plum puddings will soon be eaten, but I wonder whether they will be replaced, for I am told there is a shortage of dried currants this year!

8th December Still no sign of the Germans, so maybe they are feeling the cold as well as us. At any rate, their continuing absence is allowing Olive to get on with her painting and I spent another morning in the ice chest while the artist busied herself behind her easel.

The portrait is taking shape and I am being portrayed in my black flying overalls and wearing the brightly coloured orange scarf I was given by my German opponent. Olive says she likes the colour of it. She is painting the background just as it is in the studio, with a number of finished portraits standing behind the sitter. It should be good, for many are of nudes!

The squadron was released in toto today, the first time this has happened since mid August, so there was a good turn out for Pat Lyall's funeral which was held in the Crematorium at Brighton. Pat's mother wanted the service to be held in the South so that his colleagues could attend. We found three new pilots had turned up when we got back to camp and also that Cyril Babbage's Commission had come through.

10th December As things are so quiet at the moment, Jack is agreeable to me taking a couple of days off to see how the Mother-To-Be is getting on in Glasgow. I flew north in a Spitfire to save time, especially as the weather man had assured me that conditions en route were fair. Once started however, I did not think so much of his prognostications as there was rain and low clouds along the entire route and I had to scrape into Catterick to refuel on the way. Having been taught to fly in Scotland, I was well aware that clouds there have a nasty habit of being stuffed with mountains so, low cloud or no low cloud, I determined to remain below them for the rest of the journey. Thus I completed the trip by Bradshaw, as it is called, by following railway lines to the Solent Estuary, after which I crept round the coast via Dumfries, Stranraer, Girvan and Ayr to arrive at Abbotsinch just as night was falling. The Navy has taken over our old station, which has been renamed HMS something or other, and the place is now swarming with sailors and Wrens, all sporting wee round hats and saluting each other like mad!

Margaret was surprised to see me, for I had not let her know I was coming. But her amended outline suits her and there is now no hiding the fact that Johnstone Sprog, Mark One, is on its way! I was glad to get out of my flying boots, for I forgot to bring my shoes in my hurry to get away!

12th December Had an excellent flight back a couple of days ago, lunching at Church Fenton on the way. Thirty five minutes for the first leg and the same for the second, which was a bit better than the outward journey!

The squadron was in action over Dover yesterday for the first time for ages. However I am afraid the boys were on the receiving end (maybe they are rusty) and failed to add anything to the bag. Jake Eady got clobbered and was lucky to get his aircraft on to the ground more or less in one piece, as part of a mainplane had been shot away in the air. The rest of it parted with the fuselage when he hit the ground, wheels up, and travelling fast and two grazing sheep got in his way as the Spitfire slithered across the field. Jake apologised for the fact that not enough mutton was left to augment our rations of meat!

Fred Nancarrow, the newspaper reporter I had met in Glasgow, turned up to get material for an article about 602 Squadron for publication in the *Bulletin,* but before he had time even to sharpen a pencil, a signal came in with news that the squadron will be moving to Prestwick on Saturday, so he got a better scoop than he had anticipated. The signal also told us that 610 Squadron from Acklington will replace us here and that we are to be given air transport to help with the move.

Naturally the news has stimulated a lot of excitement and discussion, for not everyone is enraptured with the new venue as most of our replacement aircrew members live in England. However the ground crews are delighted, for there has not been the same turbulence among them and I think Command has been very thoughtful to let us get nearer home in time for Christmas. I, for one, am very pleased.

Suddenly there is much to be done in a very short space of time – packing up (Cracker's job to supervise this), papers to be sorted through, reports to be written, farewells to be said, portrait to be completed (must ring Olive), next week's party to be cancelled, time to be found to call on Barbie and Euan and arrangements to be made to return all the pieces of furniture to their rightful owners. Mr Motto is threatening to desert the unit if the cuspidors are not disposed of too! On reflection, it would probably make life a lot more simple if we just stayed on at Westhampnett!

14th December We are to exchange aircraft with 610 Squadron at Acklington before flying on to Prestwick, as our machines are more modern and have better equipment in them. I use the future tense as I had confidently expected to be writing this entry from our Scottish base, with the handover having been carried out in a nice, tidy, fashion. But not a bit of it!

By dint of working round the clock, we succeeded in completing the daunting schedule more or less on time. The advance party left by train yesterday afternoon, the bulk of our heavy stores were loaded on to a special train at Chichester station, the farmhouse was stripped of its furnishing, two Harrows were loaded with our front line equipment, Olive finished the portrait, we said our sad farewells at Lavington, I saw off the main party from Chichester station, the Squadron was released from operations (just as well, for the starter batteries had gone off in the train!) and the rain continued to teem down. Then, having got ourselves ready to take off for the flight to Acklington, the move was postponed because of the appalling weather!

As our camp beds had been sent in the train, Mickey and I have cadged beds at Lavington for the night!

16th December It has rained continuously for the past two days, during which we have sat disconsolately at dispersals, not daring to leave them during the hours of daylight in case there should have been a let-up in the weather. Sixteen Spitfires and two Harrows parked outside, dripping. Sixteen pilots sitting inside, cursing! I suggested to Group that the two squadrons might travel by rail as the forecast was not exactly encouraging, but it met with no enthusiasm. As it happened, the weather did lift about midday yesterday, when we saw the tops of the trees for the first time in forty eight hours and I was misguided enough to say we would have a shot a getting through. I regretted the gesture as soon as the Harrows took off and were immediately swallowed up in the clouds. However, we staggered off the ground a few minutes later and managed to form up into some sort of formation over the sea but, as soon as we turned inland found ourselves nipping in and out of the cloud base around 200 feet, so I brought the boys straight back into Westhampnett. It was no fun dodging around like that with so many inexperienced pilots in the formation; nor was I surprised to find that one of the Harrows had also returned before us.

The fellows had no sooner made their arrangemens to be accommodated for the third night running when we were ordered to travel by train after all! So it was another mad rush to the telephone to cancel the bedding arrangements just made, by which time three buses had arrived to transport us to London to pick up a train there. We were on the road at last – or so we thought! We were stopped by the police on entering Midhurst when I was handed a message from Group Headquarters telling me that, as the weather was definitely going to improve overnight, all of us were to return to Westhampnett to prepare to fly north tomorrow! What a palaver!

It would have been too embarrassing to have rung up yet again; we just turned up at Lavington to find Barbie not in the least surprised to see us! In fact, our beds had not been stripped!

17th December The Met man got it right this time! Conditions were much improved this morning and a predicted tail wind along the whole route would have allowed us to make Acklington in one hop, without the bother of landing en route to refuel. Thus prepared, we took off almost unnoticed, everyone having long since lost all interest in our departure, and climbed through broken cloud and set course for Acklington in good visibility. We were really on our way at last.

However, the crystal ball let our Met man down for, after flying for half an hour, it was obvious we were not making the progress we should and that our promised tail wind had done an about face and was slowing us down considerably. So we had to make a refuelling stop after all. A glance at the map showed me that Catterick was conveniently placed and, after a vain attempt to call Control to warn them, arrived over Catterick where we were given an immediate signal to land. No Station likes to have sixteen Spitfires arrive unexpectedly and I was therefore surprised and delighted when we were immediately marshalled to the refuelling point where a fleet of refuelling bowsers was lined up ready to pump in the petrol. Furthermore, the Duty Officer was there to greet us with a bus to take us to the Messes where, he said, lunch was ready. We could hardly believe our luck.

During coffee, and after an excellent lunch, the still of the afternoon was disturbed by the noise of another sixteen Spitfires joining the circuit, when our hosts jumped up to look out of the window.

'You *are* 603 Squadron, aren't you?', they asked, when it transpired that George Denholm, who was bringing his squadron north to Turnhouse from Southend at the same time as ourselves, had gone to considerable trouble to lay everything on with Catterick.

Poor George! We had unwittingly snaffled the lot! I must confess to a twinge of conscience when we were being driven back to our aircraft and passed our Edinburgh colleagues trudging dejectedly towards the NAAFI, the Mess having run out of rations!

Duly arrived at Acklington where we reluctantly handed over our aircraft to 610 Squadron in exchange for a similar number of elderly Spitfires which we finally got into the air and coaxed across to Prestwick, where we found Crackers and his gang had already got things well organised for our arrival. The first Harrow had managed to get there on Monday and the second apparently turned up just before we did.

The Squadron is accommodated in the old mill on the south side of the airfield and an Operations telephone had already been installed for our use. When I called the Controller to let him know we had finally made it, he immediately suggested that A Flight should come on state! I realised then that we were back in Cloud Cuckoo Land and told him politely what he could do with his suggestion! Nevertheless it is nice to be back in Scotland.

18th December We must have brought the bad weather with us, for it has rained incessantly since yesterday morning and we have been unable to get anything airborne. At least we have been allowed to settle down in a leisurely fashion. I have paid my respects to David MacIntyre who seems pleased to have his old squadron operating from his Station. When he heard I had no transport, he rustled up a funny little two-stroke DKW for me until my official car turns up. I don't care whether it is made in Germany or not, for it runs well, and that is what matters most!

A Press Liaison Officer called to tell me that I am to broadcast on BBC wireless about our experiences in the South, presumably about those which took place in the air! At all events, I am to prepare a script which he will call back for in a few days time, to have it cleared by the censors before it goes out on the air. As soon as he had gone, I inspected the airmen's accommodation, cranked up the DKW and puttered up the road to Glasgow.

19th December Made a point of being back at Prestwick before nine o'clock as I had a lot of paper work to get through. The weather had taken a turn for the better so I later flew round the Sector for old times sake. Yes, it is good to be back!

Although I was airborne for just over an hour, various things had been happening on the ground and I returned to find George Pinkerton waiting in my office, being entertained by Findlay and Crackers, both of whom had just received news of their postings. Crackers is to go off to an appointment in the Middle East whilst Findlay, bless his heart, is off to take command of 54 Squadron in the rank of Squadron Leader. This is well deserved and we are all delighted about the news. At least I was able to be more social towards George on this occasion, for I seem to remember I was for ever dashing off to fly when he last called to see us at Westhampnett last summer.

Progress on the broadcast script is slow for I am finding it difficult to produce something sensible which will also be succinct enough to meet with BBC approval. Must say I am glad I kept a diary during the period! I abandoned the project this evening to join the celebrations in the Orangefield. Findlay and Crackers were both pushing out their boat!

21st December Am beginning to think that 13 Group has been taken over by the Civil Service in our absence for I have never seen so much unnecessary bumff floating around. Reports required on this;

reports required on that. Fill in this form; fill in that one. Always in triplicate, too! In fact I am beginning to doubt whether they have yet to discover the telephone! Was in the middle of dealing with the backlog when the press johnny called to collect the script, so had to drop everything to get it completed. Was in the midst of this when Donald Jack burst into the office to tell me he too has had his marching orders, and would I do something about it for God's sake! When he told me he is posted as a Staff Controller at Group Headquarters, I immediately undertook to do so!

Was called to stand-by at 1.30 this morning when a raid was reported to be approaching Glasgow from the East. However, it was dealt with by the boys from Drem and I was not required to get airborne. I flew to Newcastle later in the day, however to attend a conference of Squadron Commanders called by the AOC. Unfortunately Birdie is no longer there, his place having been taken by Jock Andrews. However Birdie is still in the business, having recently taken over as AOC 12 Group.

The conference produced nothing new and was mainly about the need for maintaining flying discipline and keeping up with our training programmes. George Denholm was there, but greeted me rather coldly! I hardly liked to ask him what sort of lunch 603 had had at Catterick!

Hector MacLean hobbled down from Glasgow to spend the evening with us in the Orangefield, but his leg is still giving him a lot of trouble and he fears he may have to have more of it taken off.

23rd December The spirit of Christmas is upon us and none of the lads is very keen to fly. However, with the AOC's strictures still fresh in my mind, I got them together to run over the revised schedules which I had brought back with me from Group. What with the mass of forms and the large wall chart which all have to be kept fully up-to-date, one wonders how we ever survived those last few months in the South! At all events, a few of the lads got into the air and I went up with them on a couple of occasions, practising the same old things, but arranged in a slightly different order. I fear it seems very humdrum after the excitement of the past few months!

Our wives have turned up to spend Christmas at Prestwick and I took time off this afternoon to take Margaret shopping in Ayr. We also took in a film and went to see Laurel and Hardy in *Saps at Sea*. Had a quiet evening in the hotel where Amy Johnson joined us for dinner. Amy is serving in the Air Transport Auxiliary and has come up to collect an Oxford Trainer for delivery to an airfield in the south. She says she wants to get back before Christmas, but I fear the weather may stop her. The forecast is not good.

25th December As predicted, a thick fog blotted out the airfield all day yesterday, which is unusual for this part of Scotland, but it was sufficient to prevent Amy from getting away, to her annoyance but to our delight. My mother and father came from Glasgow to spend Christmas and were invited to a cocktail party in the Officers' Mess and later to a dance which Scottish Aviation was holding in their new factory. This was a merry occasion with lots of paper streamers hanging from the cross beams and with lots of beer being spilled on the floor! The Season is truly upon us, for we became involved in yet another party in The Orangefield on our return and it was well into the wee sma' hours before we could get to our beds.

Christmas Day, not surprisingly, started with a monumental hangover, with a fried egg leering at one from the breakfast table whilst an embarrassing exhange of presents was made in an atmosphere of forced gaiety! However, things perked up somewhat once we had had a few hairs of the dog at the Sergeants' Mess before going on to do the traditional business of serving the airmen's Christmas Dinner, at which I seemed to become the number one gravy ladler. Thereafter, once I had wiped most of the gravy stains from my uniform, Margaret and I drove my parents to Glasgow and went on to face our own Christmas dinner at her family home. And now, over-fed, over-wined and just about on my last legs, I have come to the belated conclusion that I am not really much of a Christmas man!

28th December The festive spirit is still in the air, for Scottish Aviation threw another party, this time being given by those ex-members of 602 Squadron now working for the company, to which all present members of the unit were invited. Mac was obviously the prime mover, but it was a delightful gesture which was much appreciated by us all. In spite of the social nature of the calendar, we have also put in a good deal of flying, between courses as it were, and are already ahead with our training schedules. However we are finding that a number of new pilots are being posted to other squadrons as soon as we bring them anywhere near operational standard, thus making the unit more like an OTU than a front line fighter squadron. At any rate, we have managed to avoid having any breakages so far!

Douglo Hamilton flew from Turnhouse on Friday with a plan to set up an Operations Room in the West. I spent some time with him and MacIntyre discussing the project and Mac reckons there is a large house nearby which is now empty and might fill the bill. He promised to have enquiries made and to report later. In the meantime Mickey and I called on the Ack-ack boys at Stevenston and arranged to run air co-operation exercise with them from time to time, as we can fit them in easily with our training programme.

Amy did not get away until this afternoon and I drove her to the tarmac to see her off. I still find it strange to watch a girl piloting a Royal Air Force aeroplane!

31st December Mac took me to look over Rosemount, which is a fine house set among trees in its own spacious grounds and it is situated only a mile away, on the Kilmarnock road. It would make an ideal location for an Operations Room, so I telephone Douglo, who flew over in his Hornet Moth to see for himself. He agreed with my assessment of the place.

Paid a quick visit to Glasgow to lunch with the Lord Provost who is full of schemes for raising money for the Squadron Fund, among them being to persuade Fred Nancarrow to write a book about the unit and for the proceeds from it to be given to the Fund. Margaret came to Glasgow with me as she wanted to shop around for baby wool!

The Secretary of State for Air, Sir Archibald Sinclair, looked in to see us on his way north for Hogmanay. He told me he had seen Euan Wallace a few days ago, but that news of him was grim. He is very ill indeed and is not expected to recover. Poor Barbie.

At least I am on my feet at the end of 1940! It has been an eventful year in many ways and much of interest has been packed into it. In fact, it may well turn out to have been a very significant year – who knows? But I was determined I was not going to be caught with my pants down at the end of it. This time I went to the loo in plenty of time to greet The New Year in a more suitable fashion!

Epilogue – 1975

I remained in command of 602 Squadron until April 1941, when a bout of pneumonia, contracted through wading waist high into icy seas in an endeavour to reach a Beaufighter which had crashed on the approach to Prestwick, compelled me to come off flying for a spell. However the first four months of the year were not without incident and the squadron was involved in several night attacks by the German Air Force on targets on Clydeside as well as providing the flying scence for a film being made by Twentieth Century Fox, entitled *A Yank in the RAF*! Strangely enough, the same scenes kept cropping up in a number of other films made at the time – *Battle of Britain, Dangerous Moonlight* and *Mrs Miniver* among them – so presumably someone must have done well out of our efforts as actors!

By the time I handed over to John Kilmartin, all the pre-war Auxiliary pilots had been posted from the squadron and henceforth there was nothing to distinguish the unit from any other Fighter Squadron flying in the Command. However it continued to fly with distinction throughout the war, first from bases in the South of England and later from airfields on the Continent. Many well known names commanded the unit – Al Deere, Paddy Finucane and Pierre Clostermann to name but three – and it was a proud

moment for the people of Clydeside when 602 reformed at Abbotsinch after the war and continued to serve the country until, in
common with the other squadrons in the re-titled Royal Auxiliary
Air Force, it was disbanded in 1957 and the Colours laid up in
Glasgow Cathedral. I had received a Permanent Commission by
this time and was serving abroad.

I am sad to relate that my post-war duties with the RAF caused
me to lose touch with many who shared those thrilling days of 1940.
However I still hear from others and it may be of interest to know
how they have fared. It may also be of interest to know what
happened to some of those whose names appear throughout that
diary of 1940.

AITKEN Max Aitken served throughout the war with great
distinction and has continued to do so in a different field ever since.
He forebore the title when his father, Lord Beaverbrook died, but
succeeded him as head of the Beaverbrook Press.

ATCHERLEY Dick Atcherley, and his twin brother David, were
legendary figures in the RAF. David went missing from a flight in a
Vampire over the Mediterranean Sea after the war, but Dick went
on to become Air Marshal Sir Richard Atcherley, Commander-
in-Chief, Flying Training Commando before his death in 1970.

BABBAGE Cyril Babbage became a Regular Officer in the RAF
and he had reached the rank of Wing Commander when I last met
him some years ago.

BARTHROPP Paddy Barthropp served on for some years before
leaving the service to start up in business in London. He is now
head of a highly successful car-hire firm and I am pleased to say I
meet him regularly.

BORET Jack Boret retired from the RAF shortly after the war
ended and spent his last years in retirement at his home in
Cornwall. His last appointment in the service was as AOC Norway.

BOYD Findlay went through a rough patch after the war ended, when a farming venture got into financial trouble. However, buoyant as ever, and with a little help from the Squadron Fund, he soon made his mark as an hotelier in the Isle of Uig. He died suddenly earlier this year year at the age of 57.

BROADHURST Harry Broadhurst went on to become an Air Chief Marshal and joined the Board of Hawker Siddeley Aviation when he retired from the service.

CRERAR Finlay Crerar left Aberdeen after the war and settled in Middlesborough where he became a partner in a steel foundry. I saw a lot of him in the mid fifties, but regret to say he was struck down with a heart attack shortly after.

CROSS Bing Cross recovered from his nasty experience when *Glorious* went down and retired from the RAF as Air Marshal Sir Kenneth Cross, having held many senior appointments, among them that of Commander-in-chief, Transport Command.

DENHOLM George speaks to me again and is still running the family business in Bo'ness, near Edinburgh.

DOUGLAS None heard from Crackers after he went off to his posting in the Middle East.

DOWAR Ghandar Dowar carried out his threat to raise the matter of the shooting at Dyce in The House of Commons, but as we ourselves heard no more about it, can only assume it was not taken too seriously. Mr Dowar died many years ago.

FARQUHAR Douglas emigrated to South Africa soon after the war and became a successful fruit farmer. He died in the middle sixties.

GILLIAT Virginia married Sir Richard Sykes in 1941 and went to live in Yorkshire. Sadly, she died in 1970.

GRANT   Alastair Grant returned to his native Inverness where he has carried on in his profession as an architect.

HAMILTON   The premier Duke of Scotland and Hereditary Keeper of the Keys. Douglo hit the headlines when Hitler's deputy, Rudolf Hess flew to Scotland in 1941 bent on conferring with him. By coincidence, I happened to be serving with Douglo at Turnhouse at the time. He died during minor surgery two years ago.

JACK   Donald returned to his family business in Glasgow.

MACLEAN   Hector is now the senior partner of a well-known firm of solicitors in Glasgow. His leg continued to give trouble and he had to undergo further surgery on it.

MOODY   No trace has ever been found of either Harry or his aircraft and we can only presume he crashed into the Thames Estuary during the battle on 7th September 1940.

MOUNT   Mickey served in several theatres during the war and won a DSO during the North African Campaign. He eventually retired from the RAF in the rank of Air Commodore and is now practising as a solicitor in the South of England.

NANCARROW   Fred Nancarrow wrote his book *Glasgow's Fighter Squadron* as promised and the profits from it were donated to the Benevolent Fund. Shortly after its publication he was covering a story about Coastal Command when the Sunderland he was flying in crashed in the Atlantic, and Fred was killed.

NICHOLSON   Nick won the only Victoria Cross gained by a pilot in Fighter Command during the war. He was later killed on Operations.

PARK   I joined up with Keith Park again in 1942 when he was the AOC in Malta. He returned to his native New Zealand shortly after the war and died early in 1975.

PINKERTON   George still runs his rhubarb farm in Renfrewshire.

REID   My Best Man. George was killed in North Africa not long after his own marriage in 1942.

RITCHIE   Glyn Ritchie went missing while flying with 602 Squadron over North France in the winter of 1941.

ROBINSON   Marcus still runs the family timber business in Glasgow. He became Commanding Officer of 602 Squadron when it reformed at Abbotsinch after the war. A past Chairman of The Lowland TAVR Association.

SAUL   Birdie retired from the RAF towards the end of the war after being AOC Egypt for a while in 1942. He and Claire returned to Canada where they both died some years ago.

URIE   Dunlop is a partner in the same firm of solicitors as Hector MacLean. He and his wife now live in Helensburgh where he has become a leading light in Clyde yachting circles.

WALLACE   Euan died early in 1941 and Barbie has remarried. Three of the four sons were killed in action and only Billy survives.

WEBB   Paul Webb continued to serve in the RAF after the war. The last time I heard from him he was the Air Attache in Turkey, but that was some years ago.

INDEX